Contents

The
TOASTMASTER'S MANUAL

Edited by

HAROLD W. DONAHUE

President,
The
Advertising Affiliation

MAXWELL DROKE, *Publisher*

INDIANAPOLIS

First Printing, April, 1937
Second Printing, August, 1937
Third Printing, October, 1937
Fourth Printing, January, 1938
Fifth Printing, March, 1938
Sixth Printing, June, 1938
Seventh Printing, June, 1945

Printed in the United States of America
by the Hudler Press, Noblesville, Indiana

THE TOASTMASTER'S MANUAL

A Confidential Chat with the Man
Behind the Meeting

A newspaper correspondent once appealed to the French military genius, Marshal Joffre, "Will you tell me, Marshall, who really did win the battle of the Marne?"

"I can't answer that," replied Marshal Joffre, "but I can tell you that if the battle of the Marne had been lost the blame would have been on me."

To most of us this may be just another good story. But to one man in every group it will conjure memories of many a harrowing personal experience. He's the man behind the meeting, convention, banquet, luncheon or what are you having. He knows that if the affair is a sparkling success, there will be a plethora of participants, each eager to snag a share of the credit. But if, as occasionally happens, the event is something short of a sensation, there will be voices heard in the hall. Voices with a strangely unanimous chant of condemnation. The Brothers will be saying, one unto another, that Edgar should have done this; Edgar shouldn't have done that. Well, old Edgar is certainly slipping!

So this, then is a guide book for Edgar. A manual of information and inspiration for the man behind the meeting.

Edgar will need no psychic sense to divine that the finger is on him   The knowledge that he is It can scarcely be classified as hot news. He may be the hard-working secretary of a trade association; the superintendent of a Sunday School; a sales manager on the eve of an annual convention; the president of a luncheon club; the toastmaster at a banquet of the alumni association. Or he may be merely a private in the ranks, aspiring to no high office, with no portfolio or pretensions.   Just a natural-born worker, who runs the show from the side-lines. But in any case, he is a goat. He knows he is a goat. He is a man of sorrow and acquainted with grief. At the first tentative suggestion of "Let's—" Edgar knows doggoned well that it will be up to him to carry the burden of the load. Every new plan or project, started with enthusiasm and hearty hip-hurrahs, always concludes with Edgar picking up the pieces and putting them together into something that will tick—and click. It's his destiny. He may gripe, growl and grumble. But deep down in his heart, he knows there is no escape. He can't get out from under. And if he is a real executive, he doesn't *want* to. He gets a greater genuine thrill out of a smooth running performance than out of any other one thing in the world. You can't explain Edgar by any sort of rational reasoning. He's inexplicable. I ought to know, for I am an "Edgar." Always have been. Always will be.

If you belong to our select fraternity, you'll understand. If you don't—well, then I guess this book just isn't for you.

Edgar asks for no sympathy. But gosh! how he does need help! He needs it no matter how smart he is. Whether he has been through the baptismal fire of a thousand banquets, or is just now palpitatingly planning his first Big Event, really isn't a matter of much moment. For each occasion brings unfailingly its quota of new problems and new decisions. In the ears of Edgar rings eternally the plaint of the old Negro spiritual, "It's me, O Lord, a-standin' in the need of prayer."

There are perhaps a hundred excellent volumes on the Art of Public Speaking. Countless collections of toasts, jokes and anecdotes. All manner of material to aid the orator in his worthy mission of stirring the hearts —and hands—of his audience. But nowhere—nowhere in print—have I been able to find a single adequate text book for the man *behind* the meeting. The executive looks in vain for a volume that deals clearly and simply with the *business* of "putting on a good show." A tome that tells *what* to do and *how* to do it—a book that reminds us repeatedly of the thousand things that *must* be done before the descending gavel brings a meeting to order.

Because I can find no such book I am, in all humbleness, writing this one. I am putting on paper the things that I have learned from long and varied experience. The secrets I have gleaned from many another worker in the vineyard. I hope that you may find the record helpful.

First, then, let us emphasize one paramount point: *You are the "head man."* Whether you like it or not, you are the appointed and anointed one. You may as well accept the situation as gracefully and graciously as possible. The responsibility will be thrust upon you, anyway. In every event, from a box supper at the Township school to the four-day sessions of a national convention, there must be some one individual to give orders and direct proceedings. The theory of divided responsibility simply doesn't work out in actual practice.

You'll have your lieutenants, to be sure. And if you are shrewd and cautious in your selections (we'll have more to say on this point in a later section) these individuals can be a great help and a powerful bulwark of strength to you. But after all, a lieutenant cannot, in the very nature of things, do the work of a general.

You are in command. You are in command as truly and as completely as is the captain on the bridge of a great ocean liner. If you are to bring your ship safely and smoothly into harbor you'll need all of the patience, tact, diplomacy and assorted talents of leadership you can muster up. And the first step, as we have said, is to *accept* your responsibility. Three don'ts to remember, always:

> *Don't vacillate!*
> *Don't procrastinate!*
> *Don't delegate the duties that are rightfully yours.*

Certainly you aren't going to be a petty tyrant or an austere autocrat. You're far too smart for that. But you are going to accept your rightful place as the "head man", and by your attitude and assurance lead others naturally to an acceptance of it. If anyone ever devises a coat of arms for this peculiar family of ours, it will undoubtedly feature an iron hand encased in a glove of smoothest velvet.

From the very first, there will be decisions to be made. Make them promptly and definitely. Let me repeat that for the sake of emphasis: *Make them promptly and definitely*. No one thing can cause you more trouble than an indefinite, evasive attitude. Let every man who works with you, from the humblest to the highest, know precisely where he stands and what is expected of him.

You will make mistakes. The man who never makes a mistake never makes much of a mark in any appointed task. When Roosevelt The First ascended to the Presidency of the United States he said: "If my judgment is proved sound on 75 per cent of my decisions, I shall count this administration a success." And a generation later, Roosevelt The Second echoed that sentiment when he said: "These plans are the fruit of mature reflection. We believe in them. But they may not work. If they fail, we shall try something else." It was Dale Carnegie, you remember, who pointed out, "If you can be *sure* of being right only 55 per cent of the time, you can go down to Wall Street, make a million dollars a day, buy a yacht, and marry a chorus girl." Since nine out of every ten speculators eventually part with their nether garments, the chances of being right even *half of the time* would appear rather remote.

So don't be cowed by the possibility of making a few assorted mistakes and mis-steps. Go right ahead and do the thing which, at the time, seems to you to be the best move. And do it without delay. An angel with 14-karat gold wings could do no more.

Another fundamental point to get firmly in mind is that your job begins days, weeks, perhaps even months before the actual occasion. The secretary of a powerful trade association threw considerable light on this point in a talk I once had with him. I had remarked that he probably was occupied with plans for the annual convention, to be held within a fortnight. "Yes," he replied, rather grimly I thought at the time, "yes, I am working on convention plans, and I *have* been working. Our official program, you know, says that the convention begins on the morning of October 16. But for me a new convention starts the moment the old one adjourns. In fact, even while the sessions are going on, I'm already planning for next year; noting the mistakes we have made; effecting improvements; contacting speakers for another season, and doing a hundred and one other things that will be reflected in subsequent convention programs." Yes, the man behind the meeting is about as accurate a personification of perpetual motion as you're likely to find in a day's journey.

Well, so much, then, for the generalities. Now, let's take up some of your specific problems and discuss them in greater detail.

I

How to Select and Work with Committee Chairmen

A General Chairman is known by the Chairmen he selects to head his various committees, and by the tact and skill he employs in working with these men toward a common goal. Look over the field very, very carefully. Make a detailed study of your available man-power. Consider the possibilities and limitations of each individual. Then make it the first and foremost order of business to see that every man is placed where his talents can be most productively employed. The good general will do this instinctively, and as a matter of course. No shrewd chairman would think of selecting a pronounced introvert to head the Greeters Committee—any more than he would try to fit a jovial, fun-loving extrovert into some obscure routine post where he would have no opportunity to exert his genius for good fellowship.

Very often the occupation and past experience of an individual will indicate quite clearly the post for which he is best fitted. Let's say, for example, that you are selecting a Publicity Chairman. Publicity is an involved and highly specialized business. And the matter of getting proper publicity for your meeting is of great importance. An inexperienced man in this spot is likely to bungle the job badly; may, in fact, actually antagonize the very sources whose co-operation you are especially anxious to secure.

Well, then what's to be done? Let's see: Newspaper men deal with publicity daily. They know what newspapers want, what they will gladly print, and how to prepare copy in a form acceptable to the busy editor. Amongst your membership, you probably have a newspaper man, or a man with past newspaper experience. Then, by all means put him in charge of publicity.

Another first-rate choice for this post probably would be an advertising agency man. An advertising man is likely to have a wide acquaintance amongst the newspaper fraternity. His training enables him to tell your story in an interesting, readable way. And, moreover, it is not unlikely that his agency places many thousands of dollars worth of advertising with the local papers. While, theoretically, the business and editorial departments of a metropolitan paper are completely divorced, the fact that your publicity is handled by a recognized agency man will do no harm, and may conceivably result, in some instance, in increased consideration for your copy. This matter of securing publicity will be more fully considered in a later section. We mention it here merely to illustrate a fundamental principle in selecting experienced men to head your various committees.

A few years ago, a General Chairman for a large convention did what I consider a very smart thing. Instead of appointing one man to handle the details of transportation, he had *three* transportation chairmen. The first, a railroad man, was Chairman of Rail Transportation. This was rather a routine appointment, and the chap did a fine job.

The second appointment was rather unusual. A member of the organization was also an official of the local airport. He became Chairman of Air Transportation. The city had a population of considerably less than 100,000, but the airport man was enthusiastic and went eagerly to work. He contacted all clubs throughout the country planning to send delegations to the convention, and found that a number of the large Companies represented had their own planes. Through his efforts, seven delegations attended the convention by plane. This resulted in a tremendous amount of publicity in local papers, even to the extent of front-page photographs.

The next chairman was a prominent automobile dealer. He, too, wanted to do an outstanding job. Throughout the opening days of the convention, members of his committee, in automobiles, met incoming delegates arriving by motor, escorting them through traffic, by the shortest route to their hotels or convention headquarters. This chairman also had automobiles at the railway stations, to convey delegates uptown without cost.

This courteous gesture, at one time quite common, is not frequently encountered of late. Personally, I think that it does much to create a feeling of warmth and friendliness. I'd like to see it more generally adopted.

In forming your registration committee, why not try to get as your chairman the manager of a typewriter company or an office supply house? Such an individual will welcome the opportunity to display his typewriters, adding machines and cash registers. He is in touch with many young girls who are going through for stenography and typewriting, and who will welcome the opportunity for a few days of actual business practice. Isn't it rather obvious that such a man can do a better job on the registration desk than, say, the manager of a wholesale fruit concern? He makes his living by doing just such work every day. And if he is successful in his own business, he is certainly going to try to make a reputation for himself if given the chairmanship of this important committee.

Having chosen your personnel, the next thing is to get the men at work and *keep* them at work until every final detail has been perfected. This is no trifling task.

I do not want to seem unduly pessimistic. But we may as well frankly face the fact at the outset that much of the work which, theoretically, should be done by your committees, will actually fall upon your broad shoulders. This is invariably true, no matter how able and willing your men may be. You simply cannot say, "Harry, this is your job" or "John, I am putting this up to you"—and then promptly forget all about it. Human nature being what it is, you'll have to check and double check all down the line.

You may as well make up your mind to follow the procedure of the old Negro parson who, asked how he impressed his truths upon the congregation, replied: "Well, fust I tells 'em what I is a-goin' t' tell 'em. Then I tells 'em. An' lastly, I tells 'em what I has done tole 'em."

The General Chairman must be prepared to draw inspiration and enthusiasm from an inexhaustible fount, pouring it out in unstinted measure at every stated meeting, and between times if need be. Only thus can he hope to retain the unflagging interest of his cohorts. Many a man, capable of really good work, will take a committee chairmanship under pressure, or in the enthusiasm of a group meeting—and then promptly proceed to lay down on the job, unless he is continually prodded. Such men must be flattered, cajoled or otherwise compelled to measure up to their abilities. That's what General Chairmen are for!

But with all of your care and shrewdness, you will undoubtedly make some perfectly terrible blunders in selecting chairmen. When it becomes evident that you have picked a lemon instead of a tempting tangerine, don't make matters worse by permitting a limping lame duck to continue impeding progress. I realize that I have mixed metaphors scandalously in the foregoing. But, though the language may be deplorable, the idea is none the less sound.

Correct your mistake—pronto. If the individual has ability and simply won't use it, despite your best efforts to get him out of the rut and into the race, then absolute frankness is the only possible policy. Impress upon your man that the work *must* go on. Tell him that if he does not intend to do the job, as you know he *can* do it, you will have no alternative but to replace him. This, of course, is a last resort. It is an eye-opener that may produce the desired results. A smart General Chairman will rarely be forced to take the ultimate step.

More frequently however, you may be obliged to correct an error of judgment. With the best intentions all around, you may place a man in a certain post, only to find that he simply won't do. He just isn't the man for the job. If the chap is really trying—and in such cases, he usually is—it's tough to be compelled to oust him unceremoniously.

Why not try the diplomatic approach?

Here's the way one clever General Chairman handled such a situation: In some mysterious way a belligerant and rather surly fellow—an accountant by profession— got on the official Reception Committee. He wasn't a chairman, but nevertheless proceeded to usurp authority and make himself generally obnoxious to the others associated with him. It was clear that something must be done, but for political reasons, the General Chairman preferred not to use strong-arm measures. Finally, he thought of an ingenious way out.

"Henry" said the G. C., approaching the troublemaker with a disarming smile, "I'm in a tough spot, and I wonder if you'll help me out. Some of the chairmen are showing an inclination to spend too much money. And you know we simply must keep within the budget. Now, I need a good strong man to sort of sit on the exchequer; audit the incoming bills and keep an eye on expenses. I can get any number of men to fill your place on the Reception Committee, but I don't know of anyone else who can handle this other job as well as you can. Will you tackle it for me?"

Well, of course Henry was immensely flattered. He took the accounting post, where he really belonged, and did a fine job. A more acceptable man was put on the Reception Committee, and harmony restored without ruffled feelings.

II

How to Prepare a Financial Budget
and Keep Within It

The preparation of a financial budget is one thing—but to keep within it is another! This can be done only if the budget is sound in the first instance, and if an experienced man is given this important chairmanship.

Too many budgets are really not budgets at all, in the proper sense of the word. They are "guess-timates" rather than estimates based on a careful consideration of the work to be done. "Gosh! look at that item of $400. for printing the programs!" exclaims some member of the group. "Why, I can get a printer to do the job for half of that. Let's make that $200." And down it goes at $200, which may or may not be an accurate figure. Nobody knows what sort of a program is to be produced; the size and number of pages is yet to be determined. What artwork and engravings will be necessary? Shall we solicit advertising to help defray the cost? Nobody knows. Nobody, for that matter, seems to care. But the $200 item sticks.

That is, it sticks *in the budget*. But when the bills are all in and the final sad day of reckoning rolls around, as likely as not it will be found that the expense for producing the program totaled not $200, nor even the $400 originally planned, but a sadly imposing figure of $675.82! That's why deficits are born.

No, the budget must be *right* in the first place. It must be a budget that *can* be kept within. For that reason it must be planned by a man, or a group of men who know their way around. The budget-maker should know what expenditures are absolutely essential in order to put on a successful meeting of the type that is being planned. He should know where it is fatal to stint, and where a bit of pruning can be done without too disastrous results. He should know that $500 spent on showmanship may often be worth $5,000, in prestige and increased registrations at the convention. And the same principle obtains even if the sum allotted be only $5, for promoting a church sociable.

That is why it is practically always fatal to appoint a banker or a tight-fisted accountant as your budget-maker. In the words of Caesar, "such men are dangerous." They have no well-rounded conception of the task to be done. But once the budget has been carefully considered and definitely determined, then bring on your miser man! Set him sturdily upon the cash-box and tell him to guard each dime and dollar with all his might and main. To put it succinctly: Making a budget requires one type of intellect and experience. But keeping within the budget demands other and equally important talents.

I call to mind a certain Convention which started off with a perfectly elegant idea. They were going to have system, no end. Each chairman was equipped with a pad of purchase order forms. Every transaction from the purchase of a package of paper clips to the hiring of a hall, required an order. It was a beautiful system that would have warmed the heart of an Efficiency Expert. But there was one flaw: No chairman could resist the thrill of filling out those gaily-colored forms! Each man got the idea that he was a purchasing agent with unlimited resources. And the convention wound up with a deficit of some $3,000.

It should seem needless to add that before the Budget Committee goes into action they should have a reasonably accurate idea of where the money is coming from which they so light-heartedly allot. The total sum to be expended should be worked out in close co-operation with the General Chairman. And let me emphasize that this goes for the small meeting as well as for the great national or international convention.

Let's say the budget is set at $5,000. Then it is altogether fitting and proper that some level-headed chap bring up the pertinent question, "Yes, but where do we get the $5,000?" If the reply is an airy, "Oh that will come from our share of the registration money," or "We're counting on the ticket sales to take care of that," another challenge is clearly due. "Yes, but how do we *know* the money will come in as anticipated? And what steps have we taken to pay our bills if it *doesn't* arrive as scheduled?"

Any budget, large or small, should be underwritten by a group of responsible men; or an arrangement should be made to pay any possible deficit out of surplus funds of the organization. The one and only time to do this is *in advance*. Passing the hat amongst the mourners is always a discouraging experience.

Get your money *before* you spend it. Know precisely how much you *can* spend. Then make every dollar do its duty. Observe these simple rules and Peace and Tranquility will hover over thy abode all the days of thy life.

III

How to Advertise and Publicise
a Meeting

A local director of the Girl Guides said to me once, "We've just appointed Mrs. Plunkett as our Publicity Chairman. You know, she came to town only recently and we thought it would be such a nice way for her to get acquainted."

Wow! Well, it happens that I had a slight acquaintance with this Mrs. Plunkett. A nice little homebody; an excellent wife and mother, I've no doubt. But as a Publicity Chairman—well, I had to confess my doubts. I don't believe she had ever, in her whole life, been inside a newspaper office. She didn't have even the haziest idea about publicity or advertising. She had no typewriter, and couldn't have operated one in any case. And to top it all, there was a further grave obstacle. As a newcomer, this Mrs. Plunkett naturally lacked what we may euphemistically call "connections".

Now all this, I know, is pretty elementary to you. You realize that the Publicity chairmanship isn't a plum to be handed out promiscuously to the first applicant who happens along. But too often, alas, it is likely to be so regarded.

As we remarked in an earlier section, Publicity is a business—a complicated and exacting business, where the amateur will do well to tread softly and with great humility until he knows his way about. This notion that just about anybody can "put a piece in the paper" and attend to the various and sundry oddsing and endsing incident to publicising a meeting is nothing short of a libel on a group of craftsmen whom I hold in high esteem.

If perchance you are so fortunate as to have within your ranks an experienced practitioner in the art, grapple him, I beseech you, grapple him to you with hoops of steel—and, if need be, a little something on the side. Lacking a good publicity person in your organization, if the occasion is an important one, it may be well worth your while to go out into the highways and byways and hire yourself some talent, paying therefor with real coin of the realm. Look upon it not as an expense, but as an investment that will yield bountiful returns.

But we started out, you may recall, to discuss the fundamentals of advertising and publicising a meeting. Well, why should advertising a meeting differ so vastly from the promotion of soup, soap or suspenders?

What is the first thing an advertising man does when confronted with a new assignment? Why, he sizes up the stock-in-trade, and determines how it can be most enticingly presented to a more or less palpitating public. And why shouldn't we do the same?

What do you have to sell? Notable speakers? Instruction? Inspiration? Entertainment? All right, then, let's proceed to sell our products. Let's talk about them, not from our side of the fence, but from the point of view of the typical prospect who may be induced to attend our meeting. It's not a case of "We'd like to have you stay away!"

Let's say, for the sake of simplicity, that you are sponsoring a lecture of a fairly well known public man. Your job, then, is to sell this man, and his subject to your community. Begin well in advance to gather all of the data you can get your hands on. You'll want photographs, of course, to pass along to your local newspapers (some small papers may prefer mats, and these can usually be procured from the lecture bureau). In asking for photographs, specify glossy prints. Any photographer can furnish these and they reproduce much better than the usual dull-finished photograph.

In the section which follows, "How to Get Maximum Co-operation From the Press," we will discuss in detail the matter of preparing your copy for the newspapers. But here we want to talk briefly of the importance of utilizing every possible tie-in for your publicity. The profession or experience of the speaker will nearly always suggest something special in the way of promotion. If he is an insurance man, a special invitation should be extended to local insurance men to attend. This may be in the form of a letter or bulletin. Possibly a joint meeting can be arranged through the Secretary of a local insurance organization. This will provide more ammunition for your newspaper stories.

If your speaker is a prominent minister or educator, and his subject is a controversial one, why not interview local ministers, school superintendents, etc., in advance of the meeting? Get their opinions and work these comments into your daily promotion stories. This localized angle will greatly please the newspaper editors, and you will be assured of ample space and good position. If some of the persons interviewed take a position opposed to that of your speaker, why so much the better. Nothing adds to the interest of a meeting like a bit of good controversy. People want to hear both sides of a case.

The more discussion you can stir up in advance of a meeting, the better it will be for you at the box-office. Get folks to talking about a coming event. "I suppose you folks are going to hear Dr. Baker at the Auditorium Tuesday evening?" "Well, I don't know; we hadn't thought much about it. Are you and Henry going?" "Oh, yes; we've had our tickets for a week or more. I understand they're going pretty fast. The place will probably be packed."

That's the sort of talk that puts over any kind of an event. People want to go where other people are going. They want to attend the *popular* lecture, musicale or play. That is why it is so important for the publicity man to radiate an impression of optimism. He must convey in his advance stories, in all forms of advertising, that this is to be an event of importance; that the success of the enterprise is assured from the start.

The shrewd publicity man knows the value of working from the top. The lower strata will follow the higher-ups, but the reverse is rarely true. Thus if you get the Governor, the Mayor and the social lions and lionesses to subscribe for box seats at the opera you are sponsoring, you are well on your way to a financial triumph.

Abe Martin, a genial backwoods philosopher, once remarked, "There is more difference between an amateur and a professional than between any other two things in the world." And that holds true in the handling of publicity. The amateur, generally speaking, does not know where or how to place the proper emphasis. He talks too much about minor or extraneous matters, and is likely to slight the biggest box-office features.

The successful publicity man must have what is commonly termed a "nose for news." He must be able to recognize a good story when he sees it. And he must be a sound psychologist. Which is just another way of saying that he must understand people and know why and how they react.

This can best be illustrated by an everyday example. We may suppose that your luncheon club is sponsoring a circus, and that the proceeds are to go to a hospital for crippled children. The amateur would immediately be overwhelmed by the appeal of the crippled kiddies. He would want to run a lot of pictures of them, with stories about the hospital and its fine work, mentioning incidentally that proceeds from the coming circus would go toward furthering this fine program.

This sounds like a lovely idea. But it has one trifling weakness. This weakness is the fact that it doesn't sell tickets to the circus! It may influence a limited group who are unusually susceptible, but the general public— the people we must reach—will be rather apathetic.

Now, the professional publicity man takes quite a different tack. Instead of saying, "Help the crippled children by attending this circus," he reverses the procedure somewhat after this fashion: "Hey! this is going to be the dandiest circus you ever saw! Lions, tigers, elephants; clowns by the score, and all topped off by a huge Wild West Show. More fun than you've had for years. Come along! Bring the whole family! Make it a gala occasion! And remember, you're supporting a worthy cause. Every penny of profit goes to the Hospital for Crippled Children. Have a good time. Help a good cause!"

See the difference? We put all the "push" on the primary object, which for the moment is to sell tickets to the circus. We make the reader *want* to attend that show because it promises to be a lot of fun. And finally, we break down his objection to "spending money foolishly" by giving him an iron-clad alibi: "I'm doing this," he tells his conscience, "for the crippled children. It's a worthy cause and I really should support it." Get this principle firmly in your mind, and you will save yourself many future disappointments.

People will not flock to your hall, tent or stadium *merely* to support a good cause. *Sell your show,* and let the good cause trail along *as a justification for spending the money.*

All we have hoped to do in this section, as you can readily see, is to lay down a few very broad general principles, and make some suggestions that may perhaps prove helpful. Each enterprise brings its peculiar problems of promotion, and these must be solved as they arise. But I do want to issue a word of warning to club secretaries and others whose jobs entail a more or less continuous program of promotion. Beware of getting into a rut! Don't do the same old things, in the same old way, month in and month out. Much of the value of promotion lies in the element of surprise. Give the membership a jolt now and then. It's good for them—and for your attendance records!

It's a big mistake to send out the same form of notice, in the same way, week after week. If you had an opportunity of following these notices into office or home, you probably would find many of them still unopened after the meeting. Today a live-wire secretary in a live-wire club, if a standard bulletin sheet is used, buys his year's supply in about twenty different colors of stock. Thus a different color is used each week, and this variety adds to the interest.

IV

How to Get Maximum Co-operation
From the Press

Conventions, Sales Meetings and the like not infrequently encounter difficulties in their relations with the press. And this can almost invariably be traced to a lack of diplomacy in dealing with editors and reporters. The man who is handling publicity takes it for granted that he should get front-page position and a Number One head on every little cat-and-dog item that he chances to send in. Perhaps he may even make the fatal error of trying to dictate to the paper, or tell a reporter how he should write a story. Under the circumstances, it is hardly surprising that he fails to get what he goes after.

The newspaper owes you nothing. Let me repeat that in capital letters, so that there may be no misunderstanding: THE NEWSPAPER OWES YOU NOTHING! The weekly meeting of your luncheon club, which may seem to you of world-rocking importance is just a ho-hum in the editorial room. Editors and reporters deal continually with live news and issues of vital importance. You can't reasonably expect them to get greatly excited over a routine announcement.

Nevertheless, every true newspaper man does appreciate the importance of supporting local civic enterprises and institutions. He wants and needs the good-will of your group. If you have any real news to impart, he is quite as anxious to print it as you are to have the message circulated. Even if your story of next week's meeting is not exactly breath-taking in its potentialities, the editor will give you a break, and all of the space you deserve (perhaps even a little more) if you will just demonstrate a spirit of co-operation and a little appreciation for favors received.

First of all, you owe it to the busy copy-readers on a paper to prepare your story in a workmanlike manner. This means neat, typewritten copy, double or triple spaced, so that corrections and additions may be readily made. If you are using names, as in a list of newly elected officers, be certain—absolutely certain—of your spelling. A name is a man's most cherished personal possession. If it appears incorrectly, he is certain to raise a row with the paper. And that bodes no good for you! Be careful about the initials. Take nothing for granted. Don't trust to memory. Check and double check. A certain individual may be known in the club simply as "Plugger" or "Johnnie," but if his name is Johnathan, be sure that he attains his dignity in print, except, of course, in those cases where you are absolutely certain that he prefers to use initials or an abbreviation. Al Smith is an example of this informality by preference.

In announcing a forthcoming event, it isn't a bad idea to follow the familiar Who, What, Where, When and Why formula. That is, tell who your speakers are to be (sketching in a background of previous experience and present connections); what they are going to talk about; where the meeting is to be held; the date and hour, and finally, if need be, something about the plan and purpose of the meeting. This formula has its limitations, but at any rate it does make certain that at least the essential information will be given.

Next to accuracy, *completeness* is a paramount consideration. Be sure that *all* of the essential information is given. Don't make it necessary for a reporter to telephone · you, or some other member of the organization to check on this, that or the other detail. If photographs are to be used, submit them with your copy, and see that they are such as will reproduce well on coarse news stock. This means good clear pictures, preferably glossy prints. Do not write on the back of a photograph to be used for reproduction. This is not only an inconvenience to the editorial department, but may often damage the face of the print. The caption, or "cut line" to appear under the picture should be typed on a separate sheet of paper and pasted to the reverse side of the print, so that the wording appears directly below the photograph. This caption should be limited to absolutely essential data. Thus: "Horatio K. Baker, newly-installed President of the Hamilton Lions Club."

In preparing your newspaper story, do not strive for cleverness or fine writing. Give a simple, factual presentation. If you have a situation which you feel warrants feature treatment, it is usually better to talk it over with an editor or reporter. By arranging to have a staff man write the story or cover the event, you will nearly always get a more liberal allotment of space. The reporter or feature writer will appreciate the opportunity given him to do a bit of "human interest" stuff. In this way you will make a firm friend on the staff, and believe me, these contacts are of immense value.

If you can avoid it, do not send an identical story to two local newspapers. You can nearly always dig up some new angle of approach—a different lead, at least, for each paper, even though the information is essentially the same. Newspapers will appreciate this effort on your part, and you will, in the long run, get an increased allotment of space. Treat the newspaper fairly. Never try to "put over" anything on the editor. Never "fake" or enlarge a story beyond its just desserts. Never grumble or raise a row if a story is cut down or, for some reason or other, fails to get into the paper. And, of course, show your gratitude for favors received. A nice little note of sincere appreciation, dispatched now and again, will work wonders in the editorial room.

Only the veriest tyro will presume to write headlines for a story. Even the regular staff writers do not write heads. It is the sole province of the copy desk to decide what element in a story should be featured, and to specify the size and type of headline. Writing heads is a complicated job, varying with the style and make-up of the individual paper. Leave room at the top of your first sheet for a pencilled headline; and send the story in without further embellishment.

I charge you to bear ever in mind that newspaper editors and reporters are human, even as you and I. They appreciate and react to courtesy and consideration. Show them that you value their co-operation, and they will go out of their way to help you. Adopt a condescending attitude, or take them for granted, and you will never get very far.

Do not try to impress the editorial department. As a rule, they're a pretty hard-boiled bunch who pride themselves on their independence. Such statements as, "Mr. Whoosis, your publisher, is a personal friend of mine" will probably do you more harm than good. It is almost never advisable to go over the head of a reporter who has been assigned to your meeting or convention. The same principle obtains in trying to exert pressure through a higher executive of the paper. It is your business to get along with the men with whom you come in regular contact. Use your tact and diplomacy. It will get you results that pull and pressure can never obtain. If you have a story really worth printing, you need no letter of introduction to a High Priest of the Press. And if the story isn't worth printing, it won't do you much good to get it into the paper anyway.

It is only a common courtesy to see that tickets are sent to the editorial department for admittance to all functions, banquets, etc. If it is a dinner meeting and ladies are to be present, you might slip the reporter an extra ticket, with the suggestion that he bring his wife or sweetheart. Nearly always, when a lady is invited, a much nicer write-up appears next day!

Another stroke of diplomacy is to have the Managing Editor, Advertising Manager or Business Manager of the paper as a guest at your speaker's table, now and then. Such men are outstanding in the community, often ranking with the Mayor and other dignitaries. Their presence will do you credit—and certainly will not impair your relations with the press!

On many convention programs room can be made for an outstanding newspaper celebrity. Do not overlook this opportunity. Such an individual will nearly always make an interesting talk, and his remarks are certain to be widely quoted in the local press!

V

How and Where to Find Speakers

The heading of this chapter should have a very familiar ring to most of us! Probably a hundred or two hundred years hence, Program Chairmen will be asking, "How and where shall we find speakers?" This has been the perennial problem of chairmen for unnumbered aeons. And no wonder the poor fellows are a bit pessimistic. For every good speaker one is lucky or ingenious enough to track down, he has to take five or six who are mediocre or worse.

Pity the Program Chairman, for his is indeed a trying assignment. Only the few who are genuinely interested contrive to keep out of a routine rut. Most of the others, after a few hectic months, go dead on the job. They follow the line of least resistance, and in their eagerness to get someone in the speaker's chair, they take almost anyone who will volunteer or can be drafted. This comment applies especially to service or craft clubs meeting at weekly intervals. Only one who has had the experience of rounding up 52 speakers a year, can realize the difficulties that beset a chairman.

The Program Chairman of an annual convention has a somewhat different situation. But his problems, too, are very real. Sometimes, unfortunately, he must operate with an inadequate budget. It isn't often necessary to pay a fee to speakers at convention sessions, but in many cases it is an imposition to ask a speaker to come and address your meeting unless you are prepared at least to pay actual traveling expenses. If you cannot do this, you will have to pass up some good talent; or more accurately, the talent will pass you up, and you are in danger of garnering a crop of Professional Palaverers whose one thought in life is to get up before a large crowd and exercise their vocal chords. Such exhibitionists are almost invariably deadly dull. Beware of them!

But even though funds are limited, the case is not hopeless. A little ingenuity and an accurate understanding of human nature will often accomplish a great deal, with little or no expenditure. "Years ago," says Dale Carnegie,* "I conducted a course in fiction writing at the Brooklyn Institute of Arts and Sciences. We wanted Kathleen Norris, Fannie Hurst, Ida Tarbell, Albert Payson Terhune, Rupert Hughes and other distinguished and busy authors to come over to Brooklyn and give us the benefit of their experiences. So we wrote them, saying that we admired their work and were deeply interested in getting their advice and learning the secrets of their success.

* How to Win Friends and Influence People
 (Simon & Schuster)

"Each of these letters was signed by about a hundred and fifty students. We said we realized that they were very busy—too busy to prepare a lecture. So we enclosed a list of questions for them to answer about themselves and their methods of work. They liked that. Who wouldn't like it? So they left their homes and traveled over to Brooklyn to give us a helping hand.

"By using the same method, I persuaded Leslie M. Shaw, Secretary of the Treasury in Theodore Roosevelt's cabinet, George W. Wichersham, Attorney General in Taft's cabinet, William Jennings Bryan, Franklin D. Roosevelt, and many other prominent men to come and talk to the students of my courses in public speaking."

Many of us, like Mr. Carnegie, have discovered from personal experience that we can win the attention, time, and co-operation of even the most sought-after people, by demonstrating genuine interest in them and appreciation of their work. It is astonishing how even the Great Unapproachables will warm up and become "humanized" when we go at them properly.

Perhaps I might, in this connection, humbly venture to interpolate an experience of my own. Several years ago, I read with great interest an article in *The Saturday Evening Post,* called "Brother, Can You Spare a Thousand!" It was an account of the experiences of a clever woman in soliciting for charity. At the time, I badly needed an entertaining speaker for the opening luncheon of an important convention. I began to wonder about this anonymous and evidently socially well-placed matron. Maybe we could induce her . . .

It was an audacious idea, but I sat down and wrote the editors of *The Post,* explaining our need. "If," I concluded, "this charming lady can talk as well as she can write, we have an honor spot for her on our program." By an early mail came a reply. I knew, naturally, that the publication would not divulge the name or address of the writer, but I was told that my letter had been forwarded to her, and that if she was interested, we undoubtedly would hear from her.

Well, she *was* interested! I don't quite know yet just which of our beguilements turned the trick. But at any rate, even though she had planned a trip to Europe around the time of the Convention, she altered her plans, so that she might come to a foreign country and speak before a group of some 700 people, in order that her experience and her talks to that group might be the means of bringing happiness to many homes that needed it! I will not mention the name of the little lady here, since she is seeking no personal publicity. Suffice it to say that she is a recognized celebrity who, at her own expense, and by her *personal* efforts, has raised twelve million dollars for charity. No! not thousands—*millions.*

I cannot leave this theme without a special admonition to every Program Chairman, wherever he may be, to avoid the conventional sources, at least for a time. Go adventuring for speakers. Seek them out in unusual places. There are plenty and plenty of persons all about you, unskilled in public speaking, who still have a fascinating story to tell; a story that would thrill or amuse the members of your club or organization. Go out and line up some of these people. It is an experience in human relations that is abundantly worth the time and effort it takes.

One way is to think of a good title for a talk and then find the person who can best discuss that theme. Let's say, just as a random example, that your subject is, "Foolish Questions That Have Been Asked Me." Who could talk on this subject? A Shopper's Guide in a department store, maybe; an information man at a railway terminal; a policeman; a traffic cop—the list is almost limitless. Why you could go out in half an hour and select a person—perhaps with no experience in public speaking—but with a wealth of personal experience that would certainly enthrall an audience.

Not long ago, I visited Henry Ford's famous museum at Dearborn, Michigan. I was especially interested in listening to the various young university students as they gave their little spiels in Edison's Laboratory, the Chapel, Henry Ford's school-house and other points of interest. A number of these lads spoke with remarkable interest and enthusiasm, even though they had given the same talk some thirty to fifty times that Sunday. I know that one of those boys, with a little coaching, could give a keen talk on the subject named—and it would be one that would be long remembered.

The way to get better speakers is to *concentrate* on the problem. Certainly I lay no claim to unusual powers of observation, but I am willing to wager that if I should leave my office now and walk for half-a-dozen blocks through our business district, I could see three or four new channels rich in potential possibilities for speakers. Speakers who very likely would excel the usual Government man or well-known sales manager.

And now, one final suggestion, especially applicable to the weekly luncheon clubs: Many schools, through their debating clubs and the like, are developing a crop of excellent speakers. Now and then, you will read of some young man who has won medals at speaking contests. It is always well to follow these up. You may pick a winner with an interesting story.

VI

How and Where to Find
Entertainment Features

Much that we have said in the previous section concerning the discovery and development of speakers is quite applicable also to Entertainment features. With a little effort and ingenuity, the Chairman in charge of Entertainment should be able to get a good measure of sparkling variety into his programs.

Bear in mind that the value of and interest in an entertainment feature is often enhanced by the element of timeliness. Let me illustrate this point with an instance that took place only a few weeks before these words were written: A young man in our city, who has his eyes on the Metropolitan Opera—and who undoubtedly will get there some day—took part in a large provincial musical festival, and was successful in winning the gold medal in three classes, as well as a trophy for the senior vocal honors. Naturally, this achievement resulted in a good deal of local publicity, and the young man's photograph was featured in the public prints.

A local club, holding an evening meeting within three days after this furore, sought ingeniously to capitalize upon it, by inviting the young man and his accompanist to provide the entertainment for the occasion. He readily accepted, and of course a large and enthusiastic audience was on hand to give the home-town boy a great ovation. Instead of paying a small fee of a few dollars, which was all the club treasury could afford, it was decided to give the singer a lifetime pen and pencil set, as an enduring token of appreciation.

There is, in most communities, no dearth of local talent, if we may dignify it by that term. But the Entertainment Chairman of a large club knows the importance of exercising some discretion before signing up an unknown. Some are good, and many, many more are, well—not so good. It is highly hazardous to accept talent unseen, and particularly, unheard. It takes but a few moments to slip into some music studio and there have the artist put on his or her act. If you like it, you can then arrange a definite date for an appearance on your program. If you have your doubts—or if the act is definitely out—you can stall a bit, without injury to the sensitive feelings of the entertainer. A little diplomacy at this time is much better than inflicting a dud or a tedious bore on a group met in expectation of something good. It is better—far better—to have no entertainment at all than to foist something mediocre on your group, merely for the sake of filling in a few minutes time.

You begin to see now, I imagine, that the quiet, studious stay-at-home type is not an ideal selection as your man to handle Entertainment. This job requires an individual who is definitely one of the boys. He should be interested in the theatre, radio, music; attend the better entertainment offerings, and mingle with people of similar interests in the community. Thus he becomes well versed in the likes and dislikes of an audience, and also makes valuable contacts which can later be turned to advantage.

If your club is located in a city where road shows and vaudeville appear regularly, it is well to have a local theatre man on your roster, even though he be an honorary member. Very often this theatre man can induce actors and musicians to appear at your club meetings for a delightful entertainment interlude. Such appearances are of mutual advantage. They pep up your meetings, and at the same time serve to advertise the current theatrical attraction.

In arranging this part of your program, do not lose sight of the fact that Entertainment features are designed to add variety and spice to a meeting. And no one relishes too much of even the most intriguing spices. Unless the meeting is a gala one, with no fixed formal program, keep Entertainment in its proper relative position. Do not try to ring in too many guest artists at one time (generally speaking, one entertainment feature is sufficient for a luncheon; certainly not more than two or three for an evening affair.)

Have a definite understanding well in advance as to the time to be allotted to entertainment, and do not permit your artist to encroach upon the remainder of the program. If the guest is a singer, for example, explain at the time your invitation is extended that you have ten minutes available. Suggest tactfully, "You probably will want to render a group of two songs and an encore." After the encore (allowing a reasonable but not too prolonged period for audience demonstration) it is the business of the Toastmaster to graciously thank the artist, and proceed promptly with the next order of business. Only by acting promptly and firmly can you prevent some over-ambitious entertainer from taking up the time that rightfully belongs to your speaker. This action is really in the best interests of all concerned. It is always good theatrical psychology to leave an audience yearning for "just a little more." Hold your artist down to a definite time allotment, and he will be doubly welcomed at his next appearance.

VII

How to Put Showmanship Into Your Meetings

In a sense, I suppose, the art of putting Showmanship into a meeting cannot be taught. It must be acquired from experience and observation. But we can accomplish somthing, at least, by pointing out the importance of and need for it. Because Showmanship is a universally essential ingredient in every enterprise which seeks public patronage and appreciation. Yes, I mean literally *every* enterprise, from the Metropolitan Opera to the third-rate street carnival. And I assure you I contemplate no disrespect or lack of reverence when I suggest that even Church meetings may well be advantaged by the principles I shall briefly discuss in this section.

I use the term Showmanship for want of a better and more readily understandable word. But Showmanship, in its broader application, is by no means limited to show business. A good many years ago, a scholar named Durant wrote a series of "lives" of the great philosophers. They were printed, each in a little paper-bound book and sold chiefly to high-school and college students as supplementary texts. Then one day an enterprising publisher stumbled upon the series, saw that they were astonishingly well written—far removed from the usual dull and dreary tracts. "Here's something I can sell!" he declared. By a special arrangement with the original publisher, he incorporated the "lives" into a single big beautiful book, called it "The Story of Philosophy"—and began to advertise. Today, Dr. Will Durant's "Story of Philosophy" is an accepted classic. Although I haven't the exact figures before me, I am certain that gross sales must have long passed the million dollar mark.

What did it? *Showmanship!* That little word "Story" was the magic key that unlocked these treasures for the multitude. Thousands who had passed up the little paper-bound text books, were enchanted by the unfolding *story* of Philosophy. Here was a subject they had always considered dry and dull. Now, someone promised ·to make it interesting and enjoyable—really fun. So they hurried out to buy the book—at $5.00 per copy. And—here's the important point—they weren't disappointed in the purchase! In order to make Showmanship enduringly profitable for you, you must deliver the goods. You must have something to back up the ballyhoo.

But how, you ask, can Showmanship be applied to a convention, or to the meetings of a weekly luncheon club? In a dozen, a score, a hundred ways! Ways that you must, for the most part, discover for yourself, because each program, each situation develops opportunities that are not readily duplicated. Showmanship consists of titling a talk "Fascinating Adventures in Mysterious Panda-Land" instead of "Some Travel Experiences in Tibet"; it consists of bringing into your fold artists and speakers who are momentarily in the limelight (as outlined in the preceding section); of tying-in with popular local movements; sponsoring discussion-arousing crusades; doing a hundred and one things in which there is an element of real news.

As I said at the outset, I fear I can't tell you precisely *how* this is to be accomplished in your individual case (an entire book might well be devoted to this theme), but if I can at least suggest the importance of Showmanship—get you to thinking about it in terms of your own organization—I shall feel that something, at any rate, has been accomplished.

VIII

How to Assure
a Well-Balanced Program

Like a good many other things, this is much easier said than done. If you have read carefully the preceding sections on selecting speakers and entertainment features, and on putting showmanship into your meetings, you should have a rather definite idea by this time that building a program is no task to be undertaken lightly on the spur of the moment. It requires time, thought and above all an appreciation of the eternal fitness of things. Many and many a program of able talent has been greatly impaired by an unfortunate and inexcusable juxtaposition. There is a time and place for every able performer, and it is only common courtesy, when you invite an entertainer or speaker, to see to it that he has every opportunity to appear at his best.

But how rarely we do this! You have an outstanding he-man speaker for men, and then you invite some squealing soprano who, with great affectation, renders, "Come to the Fair." Undoubtedly, you can recall many functions at which an outstanding speaker put over a smart job—only to be followed by some poorly chosen entertainment which took the edge off your enjoyment. Just a case of unbalanced planning—or, more accurately, lack of planning.

It is of the greatest importance to maintain the *mood* of the meeting. Have every moment, from start to finish, move steadily on, on, on toward your Grand Climax. If, as is usually the case, this climax is the address of your principal speaker, then plan to close the meeting promptly when he has finished. If the speech has been informal, a lively musical selection may be just what is needed for the final note. If, however, the talk is dramatic or inspirational, don't risk an anti-climax. With a few words of appreciation, let the Toastmaster bring his gavel down to signify adjournment. If you must have music at the conclusion of such a program let it be a stirring march rendered by band or orchestra.

Even so great a personage as the late Theodore Roosevelt couldn't get away with the unpardonable transgression of delivering a serious speech at an inopportune time. The occasion was the annual banquet of the Gridiron Club, organization of Washington newspaper men. Following tradition, the club had invited Mr. Roosevelt, as President of the United States, to be its guest of honor. Now, the spirit of the Gridiron dinner may be described, temperately, as one of raucous humor. The speeches and skits are invariably a riotous round of political and personal pleasantries. Mr. Roosevelt knew this full well.

And none was more adroit than he in the art of banter and badinage. But for some unaccountable reason, he chose this occasion to perpetrate a memorable *faux pas.* For nearly an hour he spoke, delivering a cold, humorless preachment, a portion of which was devoted to a detailed account of his service in the New York legislature. The Gridiron members never forgave him. And to this day, mention of that occasion is likely to rouse hot resentment.

If the occasion is a festive one, then, for the nonce, lay aside all serious business. Let no jarring note intrude for "Tonight we have guests who purpose merriment." Nothing helps a humorous speaker to get his message across like a good build-up; a general air of hilarity and good-fellowship. And, conversely, nothing is more disconcerting to the serious speaker than to follow a wholesale dispenser of belly-laughs. I have sometimes ventured to believe that the Prophet Jeremiah would have been more successful in his conversions if he had sought the iniquitous on the Morning After, instead of frequenting the Hot Spots at the hour of greatest gayety. His timing was very bad.

I am writing these words on an afternoon in November. Tonight we have a club meeting. Our speaker is a celebrated radio commentator, a chap who speaks thirteen words per minute faster than any other radio star. To keep the entire meeting in the proper tempo, we have invited an assortment of three radio attractions. First, some boys who give an excellent imitation of the Mills Brothers; then a young girl who has oodles of personality, smiles as she sings popular songs, and really makes the audience like it. As a closing number, we have an accordian artist. He can render opera selections, but on this occasion he is playing two popular numbers that I know will "catch on" with the audience. Finally, as it is just at Thanksgiving time, our booster prizes are live turkeys, instead of the usual cigarettes or meaningless trinkets.

At a convention, where four or five speakers may be on the program at a single session, the order of their appearance may be of great importance. This is doubly true where, as is often the case, several more or less related sessions may be going on simultaneously in a hotel or auditorium. The delegate, of course, can attend only one at a time, and must pick and choose the attractions that appeal most strongly to him. In such cases, the Departmental chairmen are in competition with each other. Naturally, each tries to snare and hold as many of the delegates as he can.

I well recall the agitation of one such chairman at a large national convention. He had put a great deal of time and effort into working out a beautifully balanced program, and had carefully indicated the order of his speakers. The star attraction was a nationally-known figure. The other three speakers were able, and had been assigned interesting subjects, but had less "audience value." In the preliminary publicity, appearing in trade journals and newspapers, the program had appeared with the star as "lead-off" man. But the chairman hadn't been much concerned. "Oh," he said to himself, "they're just doing the natural thing; playing up a name that has news value." But some ten days before the convention opened, he had a sudden premonition of impending catastrophe. He called the printer who was handling the official program. "Joe," he said, "just give me the batting-order on that Departmental session of mine, will you?" And sure enough! There was the star's name, leading all the rest!

Fortunately, there was time to correct the error before the program actually went to press. Would it have made much difference? Well, you would have thought so, if you had seen the beads of perspiration standing out on that chairman's face! "Say!" he exclaimed, "if we lead off with that star speaker, there wouldn't be a corporal's guard left in the room to hear our other talent. Everyone would have walked out and gone to some other meeting two minutes after he ceased speaking. He was the 'bait' we had to use to hold our crowd together!"

IX

How to Begin and Close Meetings
on Scheduled Time

"Long experience has taught me how to figure an appointment with my wife," a business man once said to me. "She is always punctually thirty minutes late!"

That psychology has profoundly influenced public life in America. "They won't begin on time" is a catch-phrase engendered by bitter experience. And, usually, they don't! The few old faithfuls who naively arrive on schedule are compelled to while away fifteen minutes or half an hour, waiting on the crowd to gather. Let this happen a few times and they, too, begin to lag.

The only individual who can correct this condition is the Chairman of the meeting. It is fairly and squarely up to him. The reason meetings and sessions at Conventions do not run like clock-work is because of the fact that few chairmen have the courage to *start on time*. For years, most of us have been sold on the idea that a meeting will be at least ten to fifteen minutes late in getting under way. Consciously or unconsciously, we arrange our personal schedules accordingly. When a large crowd gets this notion, the net result is that instead of losing ten or fifteen minutes, the meeting is usually a full half-hour behind schedule.

And time lost at the outset can rarely be made up as the sessions progress. Indeed, the whole tendency of a meeting is to slip farther and farther behind. Thus we see that the Chairman's problem is not only one of beginning a meeting on time, but also of keeping it on schedule thereafter. Roughly, there are three major reasons why meetings, even though they begin promptly, fail to keep on schedule: (a) Too many events have been programmed to be encompassed within the time limits; (b) Extraneous matters, such as announcements, bulletins, etc., are interpolated without due time allowance; (c) Speakers are not held rigidly within their specified time allowance. We shall deal with the latter aggravation in a later section.

As to points a and b: Well, it should be obvious that you can't crowd more than sixty minutes of action into any hour. Anyone who is capable of mastering the simplest mathematics, should be able, theoretically at least, to avoid the hazard of an over-crowded program. But the problem is not always as simple as it seems. The experienced chairman, if he has an hour at his command, will not schedule four fifteen-minute speakers. Human nature being what it is, he knows that something (probably a combination of a number of things) will surely bob up to upset the perfect schedule. Granted that each man holds religiously to his fifteen-minute allotment (which would be listed as at least a minor miracle) the program would still come out behind schedule. First, introductions eat up time. This applause after the conclusion of each talk must likewise be subtracted from your time allowance; also the few moments of unavoidable confusion while a speaker makes his way to the rostrum. Little things, I grant you, but they must all be taken into account. So your smart chairman, though he may allot fifteen minutes to each speaker, on the printed program, has privily counselled his stable of stars, "Hold it to ten, or twelve at the outside; we've got to finish on the nose." He does this with the mental reservation that if the gods incline, and there should chance to be a few minutes to spare, it can very profitably be utilized as an impromptu recess. This idea of pausing for a stretch is always a good one, especially where the session is rather long-drawn-out. It is best, however, not to indicate the recess on the printed program. Let it come as a surprise where time permits. If the recess is announced in advance, the delegates, forewarned, may seize the opportunity to duck out for a smoke or a trip to the bar, and there is likely to be confusion and delay in again bringing the meeting to order.

I'll admit that it takes a lot of courage to run a convention or a meeting according to time-table. But in the long run it is easier than being continually harassed by a lot of unfinished business. Once the chairman proves such exactness at his opening meeting, he will have everyone with him throughout the entire convention. For, though you may not guess it by the way they sometimes lag, most folks really *like* to be on time. Their lateness at meetings is largely a habit, coupled, as we have already pointed out, by a well-founded belief that others, too, will be tardy and "they won't begin on time."

Yes, people *like* to be on time. They like radio programs and the theatre because they *know* the performance will start on time and run on a split-second schedule.

People, as a whole, appreciate such showmanship, and they admire the chairman or president of any club who has the—well, let's say temerity to prove by actual practice that 12:15 means precisely a quarter after twelve and not 12:30 or twenty minutes of one.

X

How to Gain and Maintain Order

"They were overwhelmed" wrote an observer of one of Napoleon's regiments, "they were overwhelmed by the thunder of his stentorian silence." It is a sentence which every presiding officer might well memorize and ponder well.

For we haven't, most of us, begun to appreciate the possibilities of Silence. It has a power that far transcends the most vibrant voice. Yes, Silence can accomplish miracles when words would go unheeded, or perhaps arouse active antagonism.

Ask any man long experienced in gaining and maintaining order. He will counsel you, as the presiding officer, to walk quietly to your post. Sound the gavel or gong in a firm, authoritative, but not offensively belligerent way. And then wait. Just wait. Gaze over the audience in a calm, pleasant, confident manner. Say nothing. And say it with a great deal of eloquence. I'll gamble that in about forty seconds you will be able to hear a pin drop in that room.

Why? Well, it's the old law of passive resistance at work. And it's a mighty hard law to lick. Your silence is such a contrast to the noisy babel of the room that it *impels* attention—attention *and* consideration. Your confident attitude furthers the impression that you *expect* order and intend to have it. Your silence having caught the attention of and quieted the audience, they *remain* quiet. In such an atmosphere, no one is disposed to start anything.

But the moment you obviously *try* to gain order, you arouse the spirit of conflict. Such efforts serve only to defeat your purpose. The crowd reasons instinctively, "So, he wants us to be quiet, eh? Well, we'll show him!" And they proceed to do so in no uncertain terms. Unfortunately, some chairmen use the gavel or bell with the force of a riveter in a boiler-factory. Such gestures antagonize an audience. Any undue display of force is an admission of weakness. The unseemly clatter asks, as plainly as words, "Am I going to have trouble with you?" And the boys answer with hoots and jeers. They *must* make that response to assert their independence and demonstrate that they aren't to be intimidated by any so-and-so chairman.

Pleading and cajoling, as you must readily see, can lead only to a continuation of the spirit of conflict. That's why such remarks as, "Quiet, please!" or "Now, now, gentlemen, let's have order!" are worse than wasted. The chairman has proven that he is not master of the situation. He is on the defensive and the audience is quick to perceive this. "So the noise worries him, eh? He can't

take it! Well, let's give him some more of the same!"
These may not be the conscious thoughts of the group,
but an instinctive reaction is egging them on—and the
result is equally disastrous.

Of course there is always the hilarious or troublesome
fellow who simply can't conform to the will of the majority. Rare is the chairman who has not encountered
such an individual. He, however, presents quite a different problem. We'll deal with him in another section.

XI

How to Handle Hecklers
and Drunks

It takes a courteous, and a courageous presiding officer to handle disturbing elements in a meeting. But there is only one plan which will win the admiration of a group at any time, and that plan is ACTION! If some drunk or heckler is upsetting the pleasure of dozens around him—or, if those surrounding him are just laughing to encourage him—as a chairman, I would pardon myself right in the midst of a speaker's talk (which I have done on many occasions) and would direct my remarks to the noisy individual. I have found that, directly admonished, such persons either remain silent or get out.

The foregoing applies, of course, to the boisterous individual—the obnoxious person who is patently disturbing the speaker and generally interfering with the tranquility of the occasion. Quite another type is the self-important person who feels impelled to interrupt the speaker with some observation of his own. He may be drunk, or he may be just a born publicity seeker. In any case, the speaker must handle these situations as they arise, with all the tact, diplomacy and confidence he can command. As a chairman, I would hesitate to intrude, at least for a few seconds, until the speaker has had an opportunity to answer the heckler, or until he signals, by his attitude, that he would welcome assistance.

If the speaker is obviously annoyed or disconcerted by his impromptu questioner, then it is your responsibility, as chairman, to take a hand. Arise, address the troublesome individual directly. Tell him that you are sure Mr. Blank will be glad to answer any questions at the conclusion of the talk; that this is neither the time nor place to go into the matter; ask him tactfully and pleasantly to remain silent. If he shows further indications of trouble (which is unlikely) have him removed quietly by some smiling member of the organization who can get away with such a task without notice.

I remember very clearly a trying experience of J. S. Roberts, as the newly-elected President of the Direct Mail Advertising Association. The occasion was the annual banquet of the Association and Mr. Roberts had arisen, in his official dignity, to express thanks to the host city for courtesies extended. At this point some obviously intoxicated gentleman (normally a very engaging fellow, I understand) took it into his head that he should say a few words in praise of the hospitality of the community. He arose abruptly and insisted upon being heard.

If Roberts was disconcerted, he failed to show it. "Why, hello, Jimmie!" he said pleasantly, "I'm glad to hear from you." At that moment (so I was later informed) suave, experienced Leonard Raymond, who was seated at the speaker's table, leaned over and whispered helpfully, "Steady, Jess, steady! Take it easy. There's one at every banquet!"

And Jess responded magnificently. Calmly, smilingly, he guided the intoxicated fellow through his halting remarks; led the applause when he had finished. "Now," he said, with a genial grin, "let me repeat formally what Jimmie has already said charmingly and informally. We *are* glad to be here. We *do* appreciate, most heartily, all that you have done to minister to our comfort and pleasure . . ." and so on, to the graceful conclusion of his talk. Wasn't that skillful handling of what might easily have been a troublesome scene?

This seems as good a spot as any to touch briefly upon an all-too-prevalent practice of "walking out" on a poor or indifferent speaker. I chanced to be chairman at such a session a few years ago. The session had been rather protracted, and unfortunately the final speaker had suffered from a "whisper campaign." Word had somehow gotten around that he "wasn't so hot." Thus, the wholesale exodus was well under way when I took it upon myself to arise and say, "Gentlemen! One moment, please. The next speaker has traveled 500 miles to come and do his bit toward making this Convention a success. Your company, or you as an individual, have spent good money to come here and take back some worthwhile information. So, let's forget any other engagement for the next few minutes, and wind up this afternoon session with a real bang!" It worked! The delegates sat down and listened quietly and courteously. And whether inspired by this attention or not, I can't say, but at any rate the speaker gave a remarkably able performance.

XII

Your Responsibility as a
Presiding Officer

The reason so many meetings go haywire is—to put it bluntly—because the presiding officer doesn't realize his responsibility—or doesn't exercise his authority. The presiding officer should be an advance trouble shooter. That is, he should anticipate emergencies that may possibly arise at any meeting, and know how and when to meet these issues.

At a large luncheon last summer, when some outstanding notables were honor guests, most of the ballroom windows were open. Just as the principal speaker was introduced, two large garbage trucks pulled up by the rear window, and the men started to load the hotel refuse. The noise was simply terrible. The presiding officer, his face red with embarrassment, did nothing whatever. Yet the matter could have been easily handled. A member or a bell-boy could have been dispatchd to the scene with a request that the noise be discontinued. The manager would undoubtedly have given the necessary instruction. No hotel wants its guests to be thus annoyed. Then, since the occasion was a meeting of a weekly luncheon club, the chairman might well have called upon the hotel manager, as a preventive measure, to ask that garbage collection be scheduled on another day, or at an earlier hour.

Few presiding officers take the time and trouble to station a member near the door who is well acquainted with practically everyone in the room. Instead, they will permit a bell-boy to come in with a phone message or telegram, ask four or five men as to the whereabouts of Mr. So-and-So; be pointed from pillar to post, and stumble around the room for three or four minutes (which seems an eternity to the speaker).

As we pointed out in our introduction, the presiding officer occupies a position comparable with that of the captain of an ocean liner. He has the authority and he must exercise it, to assure smooth sailing.

There is, for example, the matter of handling guest artists. Let's say you have a young singer and her accompanist. As is usual, they are to be served luncheon or dinner, as the case may be. Be sure they are informed as to the approximate time they will be called upon. Another thing: they should be seated very close to the piano or orchestra—or in close proximity to where they are to do their stuff. This would seem elementary, but you have been at many meetings where the call came for a vocalist. Up she rises, and with her accompanist, starts ploughing over chairs, tables, and past huge trays of dishes, not to mention the added hazard of outstretched limbs. All this consumes minutes—precious minutes. And what is of even more import, it robs the act of much of its showmanship and professional touch. These are just little things, but they upset an otherwise smooth-running program.

When a luncheon or dinner is over, sometimes a fork, dessert plate or a cup and saucer are left in front of the presiding officer or the guest speaker. In such a case it is up to the officer (and he can do it with almost no effort) to summon a waiter and have the table cleared, except for a glass of water, placed before the speaker. Thus, if the speaker uses a lot of gestures; if he has notes; if he drops his glasses—in short, if for any one of numberless reasons, he needs room, it is there for him.

At a meeting I attended once upon a time, the speaker's cuff caught in a dessert fork. The implement was tossed high in the air, and landed on the head of a gentleman seated near the head table. Well, as you can imagine, this caused considerable merriment. Unfortunately, the speaker was not one of those rare souls who could join in a laugh at his own expense. He was visibly upset, and it required several minutes for him to regain his composure. As a result, his speech failed to register as it should have done. And all because the presiding officer had been derelict in his duty. The table had not been properly cleared.

Needless to say, the good presiding officer has checked with the speaker well in advance, as to any special equipment he may require, such as blackboard, easel, portable motion picture screen, etc. Not only that, but he has again checked with the proper sub-chairman just prior to the opening of the meeting, to make certain that the props are actually on hand and in a spot convenient for the speaker's use.

Not infrequently the presiding officer's responsibility may even extend to the point of getting a speaker into town. Last November an outstanding celebrity was booked to speak before 300 people. The day before a snowstorm cut across country, making fifty miles of the journey very dangerous. The chairman knew his speaker was motoring; reflected that he might not be informed as to the treacherous weather conditions. Accordingly, he sent a telegram, suggesting a two-hour earlier departure to permit a slower rate of speed over the dangerous highway. The speaker carried out the suggestion—and even with the earlier start, did not arrive until the meeting was under way.

In a sense, every meeting is a one-man meeting. And the man who clearly sets the pace is the chairman. If he falls down, it is difficult for even a brilliant speaker to rise to great heights. But on the other hand, an able presiding officer can sometimes make even a rather dull speaker glow by placing him in just the right setting.

The smart chairman knows that the success or failure of the meeting is in his hands. It is all right for him to get the idea that George will do it. It is all right for him to have the idea that his executives will do it. But he must know, too, that both George and the executives have fallen down innumerable times, and he must concede that they may do so again. Even if the chairman of speakers, the chairman of entertainment and the chairman of hotel meals and arrangements are all top-notch men, it is *still* the responsibility of the General Chairman to check every detail personally, and take nothing for granted. *There is no substitute for responsibility!*

XIII

How to Organize and Conduct
Your Meeting

The first step in the organization of a meeting is to plan it well ahead. A meeting can be no better than its advance organization. As this section is being written Remembrance Day has just passed. Our regular club meeting was within a day or so of this holiday. Several weeks in advance, we arranged with the hotel where our meetings are held that during our Remembrance period the lights would slowly dim until they went out. Then a large red spotlight was to come slowly on, shining upon the Union Jack (you recall, of course, that I am a Canadian). As the spotlight dimmed away, the ballroom lamps came on again. During this period everyone in the room rose, at the chairman's request, and faced the flag, while the concluding words of Noel Coward's "Cavalcade" were impressively spoken.

At the close of the meeting, dozens of men remarked that this was one of the most impressive ceremonies they had ever witnessed. Why? Because of the simplicity and the smoothness of the performance. But this apparently effortless five-minute interlude required literally hours of planning. It was the result of careful organization. First, organization of the idea; then a careful drilling of the engineering staff. Even so small a detail as that of gaining immediate audience co-operation, required a bit of advance contemplation.

This is only one illustration of the organization of an idea. This sort of planning must be undertaken continually if the course of a meeting is to run smoothly.

As I have hinted rather broadly in earlier sections, an important feature in the organization and conducting of any meeting is the time schedule. This schedule cannot be planned at the fifty-ninth minute of the eleventh hour. It must be done *days* in advance, and a detailed time-table set up for the entire proceedings. And once the schedule is set up, let nothing disturb it.

As a presiding officer, you might profitably take a lesson from the modern minister. Most of us can remember when it was no uncommon thing for the minister to be interrupted by some member of the Ladies Aid or the Men's Bible Class, with a belated announcement. Sometimes the announcements were made orally from the congregation. Or again, a note, illegibly scrawled on a scrap of paper, would be passed up to the pulpit. The minister would then do his best to decipher the hot news that Circle No. 4 would meet on Thursday afternoon at the home of Mrs. Blank-Blank, on Cedar Street.

Yes, that is the way they used to do it. But the present-day minister has usually organized his announcements in a much more systematic manner. He insists that announcements be clearly written and handed in well in advance. They are then organized and detailed day by day, making it easy for members of the congregation to fix the various dates clearly in their minds. You might very well adopt a similar plan for your meetings.

If your schedule is a crowded one, announcements may usually be made while some members are still eating dessert. Waiters have, of course, been instructed to serve those at the head table first. The dishes at this table should then be cleared away as quickly as possible. It probably will be better, however, to leave the dishes of the final course on the other tables. The waiters will hardly have time to clear them away without delaying the program.

During the course of the meal, you have naturally been chatting with the guest speaker, presenting some highlights on the membership perhaps, which may serve to give him a better understanding of his audience. And you, in turn may have picked up some items of information concerning the speaker, which you can work into your introduction. But do not construe this as a suggestion that you should wait until this tardy moment to plan what you are to say in presenting the club's guest.

Like every other phase of the meeting, your introduction, or at any rate the general plan of it, should be worked out long before the hour of the meeting. But we'll go into this more fully in a later section.

XIV

How to Judge Audience Reaction

It is sad to relate that some men who have been speaking in public for years have given little or no thought to the vitally important matter of judging audience reaction. And a great many chairmen and presiding officers just don't know what it is all about. Apparently, these individuals are speaking only for their own edification. Such men are usually too self-centered. They are thinking of themselves instead of actively sizing-up the audience.

Reading from manuscript (which of course no presiding officer should *ever* do) is one of the prime reasons for inadequate or inaccurate study of your audience. Now and then you will find a man who can read and observe his audience more or less simultaneously. But such skill is acquired only after long practice. Most of us would never become very proficient. We are so occupied with the words on a printed page that we can think of little else. And the man who is giving a canned talk from memory is not in a much more favorable position. He is concentrating every effort on *remembering*. The audience becomes not a group of normal human beings, but merely something to speak to.

Thus you readily see that the man who speaks extemporaneously, or who uses notes, memorizing *ideas* rather than actual words, has a marked advantage. His talk is more plastic, and he can experiment until he finds himself in rhythm with the audience.

Such fortunate individuals are usually quick to sense audience reaction, although they may find it difficult to explain to others the method or system which they employ. The first step, in any case, is to really *look* at the people out there in front of you. Turn from one group to another. Observe the expression, or lack of expression on various faces. Are they interested in what you are saying, or are they more intent upon examining the millinery, haberdashery and haircuts of their neighbors?

The normal attitude of an audience is one of interest and attention. When attention wanders; when people pecome fidgety, it is a pretty sure sign that you are no longer holding them—and you had best do something about it. Don't seek a convenient alibi. The responsibility is yours. Take it! Remember, there are no uninteresting subjects. There are only uninteresting speakers. It is your business to make the subject interesting by interpreting it from the point of view of your audience.

These remarks apply more to the speaker than to the presiding officer. No presiding officer, unless he is known from past experience as a bore, should experience much difficulty in getting the attention of a group for the comparatively short time he is in the limelight. People have attended the meeting voluntarily. They presumably want to hear what is to be said, and when the presiding officer arises, that is a signal that the show is about to start. When the preliminary hub-bub has subsided, he should have relatively close attention.

But most presiding officers are, at one time or another, also speakers. And it is well to master the arts and artifices of handling an audience under unfavorable conditions. If the attention of a group is wandering, then there is only one thing to do—*bring it back*. A speaker blessed with story-telling ability can often do this by injecting an apt anecdote. Or he can relate some colorful experience or personal illustration. Sometimes a pause, or a change of pace will work wonders. If you have been speaking rather rapidly, slow down for a time. If you have been speaking loudly, drop to a lower register (a whisper is sometimes even more emphatic than a shout.) All these things are "tricks of the trade" employed regularly by the professional, who well knows the importance of keeping his hearers in an expectant mood.

XV

How to "Thaw" a Cold Audience

You needn't be either a magician or a coal dealer to "thaw out" a cold or hostile audience. But you must have a sympathetic understanding of human nature and a real desire to have people like you.

It is a presiding officer's responsibility to "warm them up" for a speaker. Perhaps he will indulge in a few pleasantries, just to "break the ice". Then, he should sketch briefly and interestingly the speaker's background and accomplishments. His whole attitude should be one of enthusiasm. He should engender a feeling that "this is going to be good. We're in for a real treat today, folks!" I say this *should* be done. Unfortunately, it rarely is. The chairman, more often than not, conveys an impression of boredom or downright skepticism. His every act seems to say, "I don't know much about this guy, but I have a strong suspicion that he is a four-flusher or a dud. Well, anyhow, it's my job to introduce him, so here goes. Let's see, what is the name . . . ?"

When a speaker runs into that sort of chairman—and I repeat that the type is rather general—he simply has to do the best he can to offset the cold shower. And he must do it, as a rule, within the first two or three minutes after

he gets on his feet. How is it done? Well, every experienced speaker has his own technique. But I'll give you
a few illustrations.

A year ago, I was asked to speak before a group of
500 college boys and girls on Empire Day. I had two
weeks' notice, so I checked up to find what had happened
on five previous Empire days. It was the same old story.
Some stupid speaker got up and talked endlessly about
the flag and country. In the immemorial manner, he
tried to choke patriotism down the youthful throat. Well,
I could imagine that the boys and girls were pretty well
fed up with that sort of thing. I could just picture them
sitting there, stubborn and resentful—a pretty tough
bunch to thaw out.

When I arrived at the meeting, I asked to be given a
chair on the platform, where I could make a mental
check-up of my group. I wanted to open with some unusual or arresting idea to get these youngsters on my side
immediately.

After being introduced, I walked back and forth
across the platform two or three times, smiled at my
group, and said something like this: "It is very interesting to me, this morning, to see that 30 per cent of the
young ladies are wearing African Brown dresses; 18 per
cent green dresses; 7 per cent Spanish Tile; 28 per cent
black. There must be some reason for this, and if I were
in the ladies wear business I would find out the answer,

so I would know how to do my purchasing, as well as a better job of selling, and not have a lot of left-overs at the end of the season. If I were a beauty operator, I would be highly elated at this occasion, because I notice that over 90 per cent of the girls in this room have bobbed hair. More than half of you have permanent waves, and most of the others have marcels. So I would know immediately the possibilities of a modern beauty parlor near your college."

Now, all this had nothing whatever to do with my planned talk. I knew they would be puzzled. They wouldn't know what to make of such an opening. And that was precisely the reaction I was after. They had expected and dreaded a cut-and-dried talk. I wanted to take them completely by surprise. I was told later that I had succeeded in getting attention to a greater degree than it had ever been gotten before. That's one way of "thawing out" a group.

Often, to thaw out an audience, a speaker will find that he must change his talk entirely; give a message quite different from the one he had originally planned. This has happened to me a number of times. Here's an illustration:

A few months ago I was to speak to a Men's Club of a certain church. The occasion was their annual banquet, and it happened that I had never been at the church before. I looked over my audience and was rather disconcerted to observe that there was scarcely a man in the room under fifty years of age. These were grey-haired veterans—that is, those who were fortunate enough to possess any hair at all. And I had prepared a talk on "Youth"! Well, it just wouldn't do, of course, And I had to do some quick thinking.

I asked the chairman how many weeks would elapse before their teams would be organized to deliver to the congregation their boxes covering a year's supply of Sunday envelopes for church offerings. I was told that this would take place in about two weeks. So I promptly devoted my talk to Sour Faces and Sweet Faces which I had met during my own canvass on church offering envelopes. Most of the men in this group had been doing that sort of things for years, and had gotten almost into a routine manner of taking "No" as a response, or accepting decreases instead of increases. I knew then that I was speaking a language—and discussing a situation—that they could readily understand, and in which they were sure to be interested. I found that within three or four minutes I had the men with me. The process of "thawing out" had been completed.

You may recall the notorious brawls and labor riots some years ago at the plants of the Rockefeller-controlled Colorado Fuel & Iron Company. At the height of this agitation, John D. Rockefeller, Jr., insisted upon making a personal investigation of the situation. He went to

Colorado; met the leading agitators; talked with them, and, more important, *listened* to their point of view. Gradually, he began to make friends among them, and as a result was invited to address the representatives of the strikers. He was in a trying spot, as you can readily imagine. But his opening remarks—his method of "thawing out" his audience is well worth noting here. "This," he said, "is a red-letter day in my life."

"It is the first time I have ever had the good fortune to meet the representatives of the employees of this great company, its officers and superintendents together, and I can assure you that I am proud to be here, and that I shall remember this gathering as long as I live.

"Had the meeting been held two weeks ago, I should have stood here a stranger to most of you, recognizing few faces. Having had the opportunity last week of visiting all the camps in the southern coal fields and of talking individually with practically all of the representatives, except those who were away; having visited in your homes, met many of your wives and children, we meet here not as strangers, but as friends. It is in that spirit of mutual friendship that I am glad to have this opportunity to discuss with you our common interest . . ."

Don't you agree that this is a pretty good example of the "thawing out" technique? Evidently the miners thought so, for the speech was very well received.

XVI

How to Make the Reading of Reports
and Minutes as Painless
as Possible

A truly painless method is to eliminate these traditional time-consuming features from the program! Make it a rule that no reports of this character are to be read at open meeting. The modern club today transacts all business at executive meetings, and once a year puts a financial report before the membership.

Of course there are times throughout the year when it may seem advisable to adopt new by-laws or amendments to existing by-laws. And to avoid the possible criticism that one small clique is "running things," these proposed changes—and the reasons motivating them—should be presented to the membership at large. Personally, I strongly prefer the plan of taking a mail ballot in such cases. If, for one reason or another, this is deemed inadvisable, then select a member who can quickly and clearly put the matter before the club, without running around the block to do it. This chap must be a salesman with an engaging personality, yet must, of course, avoid an impression of trying to high-pressure or "railroad" the measure through. Don't get a man who speaks down in his shirt, or who gives an impression of doubt or hesitation. Select a fellow who looks the membership in the eye, tells them the story intelligently, and says in effect, "Now, boys, what shall we do about this?" Actually, he decides the issue by his own attitude of confidence, but the members *think* they have made the decision. That's sound psychology.

About ninety per cent of the membership of any club go to the meetings for entertainment, inspiration, knowledge, and the making of new friendships. They don't give two hoots about business reports, so long as the club remains comfortably solvent. Clubs that try to follow parliamentary procedure—and chloroform members with long-winded reports—are in for a tough time in this fast-moving age.

I should add that these comments do not refer to lodges or secret orders, which can operate only with pomp, tall chairs, secret entrance knocks and strict parliamentary procedure.

XVII

How to Introduce a Speaker

The adequate introduction of speakers is perhaps our most neglected art. In your position as Chairman of a meeting, you certainly want to do your share to raise the standard of such public presentations to a deservedly higher level. It isn't difficult. Indeed, the art is so simple that I can conceive no earthly reason why any man should not master it after one or two trial thrusts.

In covering this subject I feel that I can perhaps do no better than to quote a length from a little book* published by the house which sponsors this present manual:

"Rising to hold communion with the visible forms before them, Chairmen speak a various language. But roughly (very roughly, if I have my way about it!) they may be divided into two classes. First, we have the Chairman who appears to labor under the delusion that he is making the principal address of the day. He piles superlative on top of hyperbole—and no orator under God's canopy could live up to half the flowery·tributes that are thrown recklessly to right and left. Meanwhile, as the minutes tick fatefully on, the supposed speaker nervously

*THE ART OF TALKING ON YOUR FEET (in the *Personal Progress Library* series) Maxwell Droke, Publisher.

fingers a napkin and performs a mental operation upon his masterpiece, removing the heart, lungs, liver and lights, in order to get by somehow in the few miserable moments that may be left him.

"Perhaps you recall the excellent story that William Jennings Bryan used to tell with great relish. Confronted with just such a Chairman—and a fixed time limitation— Bryan had actually less than ten minutes to talk. He made the best of a bad situation, as every seasoned speaker must. A few moments later, rushing to catch a train, he overheard a farmer remark to another, 'Say, Old Bryan sure made a rousin' talk, didn't he?' 'Yeh,' replied his conferee, with just a shade of dubiousness, 'Yeh; and that little bald-headed feller that spoke last wasn't no slouch, neither!'

"A fairly safe rule to follow—if you are one who goes in for rules and regulations—is that the bigger the man, the less you need say about him. People have come to hear the speaker. If he is a great deal better than you are, don't block his path or infringe upon his time. Be brief!

"In the days before Depression, when Calvin Coolidge was at his Olympian height as President of the United States, he accepted an invitation to address the American Association of Advertising Agencies, a powerful organization presided over at that time by James W. Young. Naturally, it devolved upon Mr. Young to preside at the banquet and introduce the President. And he was sorely distressed. Ordinarily a man of poise and power, Jim Young was just plain scared. How could he possibly measure up to the occasion? What could he say that would fittingly pay tribute to So Great a Man? For weeks, he worked upon that speech of introduction, polishing each phrase with loving care. Then, at the last moment, he threw his oration into the hotel wastebasket, donned his swallow-tail and went forth to meet his fate. At the precise second he arose, gestured for silence, waited for an impressive moment, and said—the best thing that he could possibly have said in the circumstances—'Ladies and Gentlemen—The President of the United States!'

"In the intervening years, James Young's formula has been followed many times for the introduction of Great Personages. But at that time and place it was a startling, almost a stunning innovation. Full half the ovation that followed was a personal tribute to Jim Young for his sheer genius in stripping an introduction of ridiculous encumbrances.

"But the opportunity to introduce a President of the United States comes rarely to us average men. More likely are we, in the ordinary run of introductions, to say too little rather than too much. The purpose, and the sole purpose, in introducing a speaker to an audience is to give him a background. It is in this that most introductions fall far short of the mark. The speaker is selected by a program committee; perhaps he is a last-minute substitute. I know of countless cases where a chairman has arisen to introduce a speaker of whom he has never heard. He has only a mumbled introduction and a printed slip, with the name and address, to guide him. This is a deplorable condition, grossly unfair to the speaker and the Chairman. If, as the presiding officer, it is your duty to introduce a speaker, don't dilly-dally until the last minute. Learn something about the man—if possible, well in advance. In the words of Al Smith, 'Let's look at the record.' Where is he from? What has he done? What is his official connection? With what authority does he speak? Get all the information you can. Absorb it thoroughly. Then plan carefully in advance what you can say that will be fair alike to the speaker and the audience.

"If you are compelled, through circumstances over which you have no control, to defer gathering your data until you arrive at the meeting, make an opportunity to talk for a time with the man you are to present. If it is a luncheon or dinner meeting, you can tactfully draw him out during the course of the meal. Avoid the appearance of an inquisition, though of course you may have to ask a number of direct questions. If, in addition to introducing the speaker, you are charged with the responsibility of conducting the meeting, find out approximately how much time the speaker will require, and do your best to arrange the remainder of the program to accommodate his requirements. If there is an ironclad time limitation—such as a one-thirty adjournment for a luncheon club, explain this condition to your speaker in advance. And he, in turn, should accommodate himself to this limitation. Incidentally, most luncheon-club meetings are far too crowded. The Chairman of the Golf Committee has a few words to say. There is a man from the City Hall who wants to say something on Fire Prevention Week. Somebody else is plugging a concert, or the next event at the Little Theatre. The Treasurer must put in his nickel's worth concerning delinquent dues. And the poor speaker who has been promised a half-hour finds that he has a word-weary audience, and a scant twenty-two minutes in which to ring the welkin.

"It seems absurd to mention this admonition, but I know from bitter experience the necessity thereof: Learn the NAME of the man you are to present. Be SURE you know how to pronounce it correctly (if you have the slightest doubt, ASK the man himself. He will much prefer to tell you privately than have you stumble and garble his most personal possession when you get to your feet.) Get the first name, the initial, the last name clearly fixed in your mind. Memorize it. Memorize the business connection or official title, also; and the exact title of the speech, Nothing is more disconcerting to the speaker and the audience than to have a Chairman pause at the climax of his introduction and consult a slip of paper to ascertain the name of the speaker. Then another pause, while he checks on the business connection. This is followed by the usual glib 'who will speak to us today—on —' (a third significant pause) '—on "Mountains and Mousetraps!"' This is a dead giveaway to one and all that the speaker hasn't made much impression on you, and that you are pretty well bored with the whole proceeding, anyway. Here, at least, is one spot where notes should be ruthlessly cast aside. Anyone can concentrate to the extent of learning a speaker's name, business connection, and the title of his talk. If you are not willing to make this small effort, then step down from the rostrum and let someone else do the honors. Your place is in the audience!

"To introduce a stranger may seem to you a difficult undertaking; but I sometimes think that to introduce one whom you know well is an even greater test. There is a temptation, in such cases, to become too familiar; to relate some incident or experience from the speaker's earlier life which, while presented in a spirit of fun, may cause him much embarrassment. Remember that the speaker is under considerable nervous tension anyway. A joke or wisecrack which might not ordinarily phase him in the least may have disastrous effect at such a time. Be doubly sure your remarks are restrained and in good taste.

"I recall a case where a man was called upon to present a speaker he had known intimately for many years—a native of Missouri. Thinking to have some fun at his friend's expense (and using exceedingly poor judgment and taste) he wound up his introduction by pointing out that Maine was noted for its baked beans, Kentucky its corn liquor, 'but our speaker today hails from Missouri —and you know that is the state from which we import most of our jackasses.'

"The speaker, a sensitive mortal, blushed furiously and floundered about in a pitiful fashion, until he finally regained self possession. It was a cruel thrust, and a very poor sort of fun. Like so many Chairmen, this chap felt that he was called upon to say something clever, when a simple, straightforward introduction would have been infinitely better."

XVIII

How to Guide a Speaker Into
Desired Channels

Not infrequently a capable speaker may fail to register with a certain group. His talk may have been excellent in its way, but in some manner he did not "hit it off" with this audience. Analyze this failure and you will find that, for any one of a number of reasons, the speaker did not understand his group. He was not completely informed as to their wants, needs or desires. I once heard a speaker, addressing an Advertising Club, build his entire talk around the premise that he was talking to men who handled large national advertising appropriations. As a matter of fact, there were not more than three such men in the room. Most of the members represented local advertisers; others were connected with allied arts such as printing, engraving and the like.

Now, who is to blame for such misconception? Personally, I have always felt that the Chairman of the meeting (or the Program Chairman, if the organization boasts such an individual) should take it as an important part of his job to give a prospective speaker, well in advance, a good general idea of the type of audience he is to talk to. And he might, in some cases at least, go farther than that, and outline for the speaker the *kind of talk* that he has reason to feel will be well received.

Let me elaborate on that thought with a specific illustration. You are inviting a college professor to talk on Psychology. Instead of leaving it to him to flounder around and discuss general aspects of his subject, why not tell him candidly that your membership represents a general cross-section of business and professional men; that they are little interested in Psychology from the academic side. They want to know how they can apply the principles of Psychology in their daily contacts. Suggest that he give some concrete examples; present ideas that the men can take back and put to work. You might even go so far as to jot down a dozen or so questions that you feel the members would like to have answered; or points to be discussed. In doing this, you are not presuming to tell the professor how to prepare his speech, or what he is to say. You are simply giving him a clear mental picture of the audience; an opportunity to prepare the sort of talk that will go over in a big way.

If your organization has specific regulations (Example: an iron-clad rule for 1:30 adjournment) or certain prejudices (Example: a hearty dislike for "speakers" who read from manuscripts) it is only fair to pass this information along to your prospective guest, in order that he may take steps to conform—or decline the invitation.

There is, as you undoubtedly know, a good deal of resentment piling up against the practice of reading a speech. Indeed, so strong is this sentiment that one powerful organization—the Advertising Federation of America—will not, under any circumstances, permit a local secretary to give a speaker an "E" (Excellent) rating if the speech is read from manuscript. Reports are sent to the New York headquarters on every speaker who appears before an Advertising Club in the Federation. The man who employs a "paper crutch" isn't asked to speak again at that, or any other Advertising Club in the organization. I would to God the practice was universal!

One luncheon club in the middle west, brought to desperation by a succession of poor readers, adopted a burlesque by-law and had it duly printed on a slip of paper, and enclosed with an invitation to each prospective speaker. It read (I quote from memory) something like this:

WHEREAS, the membership of this Club, has suffered untold mental anguish and physical agony through the action of certain "speakers" who persist in READING their dry discourses—

AND, WHEREAS, it is the concensus of opinion among our membership that no speech which is read is ever worth a damn, anyway—

THEREFORE, BE IT RESOLVED that it shall be, and is, from this time forth, the duty of the Sergeant-at-Arms to take his station at the rear of the hall, immediately following the luncheon, suitably armed for any emergency. Should the Speaker of The Day, after a few preliminary remarks, make a furtive gesture in the direction of an inside coat pocket, indicating clearly that a manuscript is forthcoming, the Sergeant-at-Arms is hereby instructed to shoot, and shoot to kill.

I am told that there has been a marked decrease in the number of manuscripts presented at the meetings of that organization!

XIX

How to Curb the Long-Winded or Irrelevant Speaker

Picture the crowded ante-room of the purchasing agent of a big manufacturing company. Half-a-dozen or more salesmen are waiting, each eager to get in and "speak his piece." But one man, just ahead of them, has settled down for a lengthy chat. Half-an-hour—three-quarters—an hour—and still he sits. In ten minutes he could have told his story and been on his way. And, unfortunately, there are speakers who are equally inconsiderate. Like Tennyson's brook, they go on forever—while an audience becomes restless, and the remaining speakers wipe agitated and apprehensive brows. Here, indeed, is one of the Chairman's very real problems.

What to do about it?

Well, to be sure, preventive measures are usually more effective than any effort to stop the speaker when he is actually under way. The first step is to see that your man understands, clearly and unmistakably, the precise amount of time that has been allotted to him. This matter of timing should be taken up when the invitation is extended. If your maximum time allowance is forty-five minutes, better play safe and invite your man to talk for forty minutes.

Before your speaker arises, the thoughtful chairman will again remind him of time limitations: "It is now 3:10. You are to speak until 3:40. If you need an extra two or three minutes to wind up, that will be all right." That's a deft but very compelling way of putting a man on a spot. None but the wholly headstrong and heedless can mistake the meaning of such a reminder. And the speaker who exceeds his time allowance when thus courteously warned well deserves any dire fate that may befall him.

A few, alas, will require extreme measures if they are to be curbed. In a long and eventful public career, I recall only one instance where I had to resort to the ultimate in chastising a programmed guest. This man was booked for thirty-five minutes, which I think is a liberal allowance for almost any speaker. He ploughed right ahead for forty minutes . . . forty-five . . . fifty. Although warned three times that he was exceeding his time allowance, he was still going strong at an hour and fifteen minutes, when we were finally compelled to ring the gong on him.

We were then in a critical spot. The audience was beginning to drift out—and I knew that meant that most of the men would not be back. The next feature on our program was a sound motion picture in color, brought to us at heavy expense, and the President of the sponsoring company was on hand to tell the story of the film. I decided it was no time for pussy-footing, so addressing the audience, I said point blank that while the previous speaker had greatly exceeded his time, it was not fair to penalize our next feature on that account. I told the men that this Company had invested $700 or $800 to bring the film to us, and asked them, as a courtesy, to remain and see it. Instantly, the crowd responded. Almost to a man, they stayed, and we were later congratulated for the stand we had taken. It seemed to me then, as it does now, the only possible course to follow in such a situation.

When a speaker has been fairly warned as to his time limitations, it is up to him to conform. If he does not do so, he should be unostentatiously warned by a note, a tug at his coat-sleeve, or perhaps a gentle jab on the shin that "Time's up!" If this doesn't work—well, then insult him you must! After all, isn't it better to insult one man, who richly deserves a rebuke, than to bore three or four hundred who, it may be, have spent many dollars and traveled a long distance to attend your meeting? One long-winded speaker on the opening day of a convention can cut down attendance at every session for the next two or three days.

XX

When the Speaker Fails
to Arrive

One speaker more or less at any given session of a Convention (unless he chances to be a headliner) usually isn't a matter of much moment. Programs are far too crowded anyway, and the Chairman is quite likely to exclaim, "For this relief, much thanks." But failure of a speaker to appear at the scheduled meeting of a luncheon club, where he has been booked as the sole attraction— well, that's something else again!

I confess I don't know why the thought of a group of congenial fellows sitting down together at a luncheon, without the supplementary aid of formally-booked chin music, should be so completely devastating. But if we may judge from the febrile efforts of a chairman or secretary, scurrying about to find a last-minute substitute— any sort of a speaker to fill the gap—a speakerless session is truly a grave calamity.

The resourceful Program Chairman will probably have a few aces (or at the very least, dependable face cards) up his sleeve for just such an emergency. He will make it his business to acquaint himself with the local situation; to know the men in his community who can be counted upon to talk at least passably well on short notice. Quite likely he will have frankly apprised one or more of these men that he is being held in reserve for an emergency. Thus, when the imported speaker telegraphs that he has missed his train, lost his job, or come down with an attack of insipient leprosy, the Chairman turns serenely to his telephone—and the day is saved.

Of course the Chairman's perpetual dread is that some day his precious system will fail to work. Some day, though he seek high and low, he will fail to find a substitute of any size, form or condition of previous servitude. And then, horror of horrors, the meeting may convene with a significantly vacant chair! The very thought of it gives him the creeps. Oft in the stilly night he awakens in a cold sweat, from a dream wherein that Vacant Chair stares accusingly at him, whilst the audience vents its scorn with boos and hisses.

Yes, it is a prospect terrible to contemplate. But when actually the day arrives, it may not be half bad. I recall one such occasion—a luncheon meeting of an Advertising Club. The scheduled speaker had sent no word, and up until the actual hour of the conclave, it was confidently anticipated that he would arrive. But the luncheon was completed, and still the guest had not put in an appearance. Something had to be done—and quickly. So the President arose and explained the situation briefly and graciously. "To tell you the truth," he added, "I have long wanted just such an opportunity as this meeting now affords. I confess that I feel, and I have a good notion that many of you join with me in feeling, rather like a host who has entertained a house full of company for a long and hectic period. At last the guests have gone! Thank God! we can relax and just be ourselves for awhile. We can talk without affectation or pretense. We can grouch and grumble and growl if we want to. It's all in the family!

"Now, I know that you boys have a number of things on your minds that you'd like to bring up—Club matters, or things pertaining to the craft. Let's take this rare opportunity for a little free and open discussion. I'll start the ball rolling with a suggestion . . ."

Well, it developed that "the boys" really did have a lot to talk about. With that good start, the meeting proceeded at a lively pace, and actually ran ten minutes over time before anyone had noticed! It stands on record as one of the most successful programs ever perpetrated by the club. And it was entirely extemporaneous and accidental!

XXI

Courtesies Every Speaker Appreciates

One reason so many conventions and clubs have a tough time getting speakers may be traced to the fact that they overlook the little things that make a big difference in the treatment of guests. If a man comes from a distance especially to address a group; if he sacrifices thirty to forty-eight hours of his time, to talk for only 43 minutes—then, he is like most speakers, just plain crazy; or else he has a heart of gold to do his Boy Scout deed.

A speaker traveling by train should be met at the station and taken to his hotel. His room should always be reserved in advance, and it should be understood that this item, as well as the speaker's breakfast and other incidentals, are to be charged to the club. This is a common courtesy that should be done as a matter of course.

If several hours are to elapse before the appearance of your speaker, he may, or may not appreciate some form of entertainment. A good deal will depend upon the temperament and status of the individual. In general, it may be said that the professional probably will prefer to be left to his own devices. Sightseeing no longer holds much of a thrill to him, and the few hours between engagements comprise about all of the private life the poor fellow has. After a brief check-up, leave him alone. That is, of course, unless he indicates a desire to the contrary.

But the man to whom a speaking engagement is a novelty may very well wish to make the most of his experience. If in the mood, he should be taken for a brief ride around your city; or perhaps, if his interests lie in that direction, a trip through the retail district, or to some specific manufacturing plant. If it is necessary for him to stay over night, and he doesn't want to retire at once, two or three friendly fellows should take the responsibility of chatting with him, or entertaining him in some way he likes.

Experience over a good many years has taught me that if a club member can slip in the next morning, and without making a fuss about it, sit down and have breakfast with the man who has put himself out to speak to your group, it is well appreciated. I recall that we carried out this idea with Elbert Hubbard II, some fifteen years ago, and to this day he still speaks of this as one of the highlights of his trip to our city.

Another thing—and a very important one: See that the speaker you have booked gets all of the advance publicity which has appeared in club bulletins, newspapers, or as spot announcements on the air. Then, after he has returned home, send him clippings of all newspaper reviews of his talk which appear the following day.

Often the speaker is asked to furnish a photograph, and from this printing plates are made for publicity. It is doubtful if such plates will be used again by the club. Why not send them along to the speaker when they have served their purpose? Very likely he can make good use of them.

In bringing a dozen or more speakers to our city during the past year, we wrote ticket agents in each speaker's home city, asking that they telephone our speaker and offer to make reservations or render any other desired service. This idea clicked 100 per cent with everyone on our program. In addition to this, we sent each speaker a complete time table of arrival and departure dates for the entire three days of the convention, so that he would know the service available and arrange his schedule accordingly.

A good many clubs and conventions have "boosts" or prizes of some sort—usually two or three of these awards are made at each meeting. We make it a practice to draw one of these cards with the speaker's name. It's ten to one he is still a little boy—tickled to death with winning, and will eagerly carry the prize home to his family.

About a year ago, we had a famous globe-trotter reporter as a speaker. I had found in advance that ham was a family weakness. So we purchased a lovely boneless picnic ham. We drew for this, and naturally drew his card, which of course was pre-arranged. Ever since that time, this chap has put himself out to praise our club.

In arranging for a speaker's comfort and convenience, don't take anything for granted. Hotels, often during the rush of business, ball things up considerably. So it is wise to have some one check up on the final reservations for a speaker. Thus he may avoid an experience such as befell me last Fall. I had traveled six hundred miles to speak, arriving at 7 A. M., to be informed that no room had been reserved, and the hotel was "sold out" anyway.

Many speakers become discouraged in their efforts to be helpful and obliging, due to the careless and indifferent treatment accorded them by various clubs or other organizations. Usually everything is centered around a speaker, to make your meeting a success. Then, why not treat him with a little more consideration? You should at least show him common courtesy, when you reflect upon what he is doing for you.

And finally, may I suggest that this courtesy extends to the actual banquet or luncheon table? Take, for example, the rather common matter of tobacco smoke. It's still obnoxious, you know, to a good many men. So, before you light a cigar, pipe, or even a cigarette, make sure your speaker does not object. It's better, usually, to let him make the first move. If he doesn't smoke, signal

XXII

How to Conduct a Successful "Question and Answer" Section

The first rule for success in any Question and Answer period is to select a live-wire session chairman; a chap who knows his way around, and has the knack of putting showmanship into a meeting. This is definitely no spot for a stuffed shirt.

Many and many a session manager has saved the day for a dull and uninteresting speaker. For, strangely enough, the man who has proved tedious in a formal discourse, may blossom out into an interesting and informative talker when answering specific questions, under the direction of a skillful chairman.

The first duty of such a chairman is to get the Question and Answer session off to a quick, smooth start. A lag of two or three minutes, waiting for some bold spirit to generate enough courage to stand up and ask a question, is a terrific handicap. This can be very easily avoided by having two or three dependable stooges well primed in advance. Determine the questions that they are to ask (queries of wide general interest, of course) and instruct them to fire at the drop of the hat. With that kind of a start, the problem usually is to keep the questioners in hand, so that two or three will not be trying to talk at once.

At a large convention, if the questioner fails to give his name and the city from which he hails, the chairman should ask for this information before the speaker is afforded an opportunity to answer. Not only is the information necessary for the official record, but often the identity of the questioner may have an important bearing on the answer. The chairman will at times find it advisable to re-state the question briefly, to make certain that the audience is fully apprised. Frequently, speakers have answered questions to front-row sitters, while the rest of the audience, not knowing what it was all about, twitched around, read programs, cleaned pipes and otherwise showed signs of lack of interest.

Let's say, to illustrate, that the occasion is a session of the Direct Mail Advertising Association convention. Some person has asked an age-worn, hackneyed question, such as, "Should you use first-class or third-class postage?" The session manager can make even such a stupid headache question interesting by immediately going back at the questioner: "Will you make your question more specific? Will you tell us what situation, or what particular campaign you have in mind? Situations, you know, always alter circumstances." The questioner then will show whether or not he has intelligence; whether his question was just a wild generality to give him a chance to get up on his feet, or if he really has something definite on his mind. Then the speaker will really have a chance to answer intelligently.

The session manager shouldn't have to be told, of course, that it is his duty to be keen, alert and observant while the questions are being fired in, in order that he, too, may get the idea of what it's all about. And this obviously goes also for the discourse period preceding the question session. At the conclusion of the formal talk, the chairman should be able to take up the thread of the discourse, with some brief, clean-cut comment on the highlights. This nearly always assures interesting activity during any question period.

As the chairman, you should make it clear that long-drawn-out questions, miniature speeches or illustrations are not in order. Keep the questions simple and direct— as specific as possible, if you seek a lively session. Encourage the mumblers to talk right out in meeting, "so the speaker and others may hear you."

A good many of you who are reading these words will have heard Charles E. Weirs, Homer Buckley or John Howie Wright conduct Question and Answer periods. In that illustrious trio we have three shining examples of How to Do it. These men are all just as interested in having the question period as successful and enlightening as the remainder of the program. It can be done, and is being done by a considerable number of session managers. If any other type of chairman is selected, then it's the fault of the General Chairman if the session is a flop. The time to prevent such a catastrophe is before it has a chance to happen!

XXIII

How to Conduct a Speakerless Banquet

Are we becoming a bit "fed up" on oratory?

There is at least some evidence pointing to that conclusion. Within recent years, conventions have found that the announcement of a so-called "Speakerless" banquet has caused quite a hit, and resulted in increased attendance. Personally, I am inclined to think that the waning popularity of the banquet talk is due primarily to the fact that in the past we have selected the wrong type of speaker. Too often at a banquet where both ladies and gentlemen are present, and the spirit is clearly one of good-feeling and hilarity, the speaker has turned out to be some dried old stick, who orates for an hour or more on a tedious theme in which no one is really interested. That's the sort of thing that has brought the noble art of banquet oratory to its present low estate.

But not infrequently the "Speakerless" banquet, for all its high hopes, turns out to be something of a flop. Too often the chairman or master of ceremonies can't resist the temptation to step in and fill the gap. He becomes a speaker in his own right with long, and not very amusing introductions of the various entertainment features.

There is one way—and only one—to conduct a successful speakerless banquet. Appoint a master of ceremonies who really is a *master*—a man who can mingle with the crowd; get into the spirit of the occasion; pull the right joke at the right time, and introduce the artists with pep and vigor. A master of ceremonies who will run everything on split-second schedule, and have no painful pauses.

Just as surely as you follow the traditional system of having some forty or fifty men at the head table, you are in for a boresome interlude. The presiding officer, for their consideration, starts introducing each man individually. And right there your plans for a speakerless banquet go high in the air! He may have pleased a few pompous gents at the head table, but in so doing has caused dissatisfaction throughout the general assembly.

I have attended scores of gatherings which were advertised as "speakerless banquets," but rarely have I found one that lived up to the advance billing. In those cases where the banquet really was sans speaker, you could plainly trace the guiding genius of a presiding officer who refused to clutter up his program with a lot of traditional but meaningless introductions and announcements. To conduct a banquet without speakers is not as simple a matter as it might at first appear. Much pressure may be brought upon you to drag in this, that or the other distracting feature. But if you definitely decide that the rank and file of your organization really wants a banquet without speakers, then go to it. Hold firmly to your resolution. If you have advertised a speakerless banquet, then see that it is SPEAKERLESS!

XXIV

How to Conclude a Program
Effectively

A good many clubs, in recent years, have adopted the idea of giving booster or attendance prizes. Experience has taught us that it is often well to draw for these prizes at the very close of the meeting. If the prize is worthwhile, you will find that practically all will remain. It is pleasant to win a "boost," or to see others going away happy with an electric grill, car heater or some such prize. That is one way of concluding a meeting effectively.

But whatever course you follow, I urge you not to be too abrupt, too callously brusque. For the presiding officer merely to hit the gong and mumble, "meeting's-adj'rn'd" always seems to be a bit crude and rude. Why not put as much showmanship and graciousness into the final moments as into the opening of the meeting? It *can* be done, you know.

When the speaker has concluded, it is of course the duty of the presiding officer (or the program chairman, if he has handled that part of the meeting) to extend the thanks of your organization. Maybe your speaker wasn't exactly a sensation. Perhaps you and other members of the group are disappointed. Well, what of it? The man has evidently done his best. Time and effort were required to prepare and deliver the message. Certainly the very least you can give in return is a gracious and sincere "Thank you." Try to pick *something* out of the talk to which you can refer briefly. Rare, indeed, is the talk so poor that it doesn't contain an idea or suggestion which you can mention in a spirit of commendation. This individualized comment lifts your "Thank you" out of the routine rut. It will be appreciated, you may be sure.

Having thanked the present speaker, why not utilize a moment or so to "plug" your next program? After all, the old theatrical stock-company manager was a pretty shrewd fellow. Recall his concluding speech, after the final curtain of *Camille?* "And, now, remem-bah, Ladies and Gentlemen, tomorrow night *East Lynne,* and on Saturday night *Uncle Tom's Cabin* with real blood hounds! No advance in prices. Come one, come all!" Emulating this able showman, you might announce, "And next week, another treat is in store for us all. Our featured speaker will be . . ." with a brief announcement of the man and his subject, "in the meantime, good night everyone. Keep smiling! The meeting is adjourned."

In other words, close your meeting as John B. Kennedy used to close his *Collier's* broadcast, with some pleas-

XXV

How and Where to Tell a
Funny Story

It is not my purpose to dwell at length upon the art of story-telling. To do the subject justice would require a sizeable book. But let's ask, at the outset, whether you should indulge in story-telling at all; if so, to what extent, and under what conditions.

Well, the first consideration is this: CAN you tell a story at least moderately well? Many excellent speakers cannot. On the other hand, there are men who, on the whole, speak poorly, but they possess a certain knack of narration that enables them to enrich their talks with pert and pertinent anecdotes. So they get along very nicely, and are sometimes even asked to fill return engagements!

But there are few spectacles more painful than that of a speaker standing up and cracking dull and meat-less jokes, because he feels it is *expected* of him. So, here's a pretty good rule to follow: Do you, in your everyday relations with fellow humans, tell stories, relate bits of anecdotes, dramatize your personal experiences? If you do, and if you have little difficulty in gathering an appreciative audience (aside from those who work for you, and are impelled to laugh as a matter of policy) then it is more than likely that you are a pretty fair story-teller, and in your public appearances you may venture to tell an extra-good story in its proper time and place.

But if you are not a tale-teller in private life—if you have no inclination or talents in that direction, why—in Heaven's name *why*—should you take on the mantle of a mime, merely because you are talking to a hundred or a thousand persons, instead of one or two?

Somebody once said that in building up a repertoire of funny stories, it is safest to take those that are either very old or very new. However that may be, by all means avoid the practice of running through the last couple of issues of a magazine of some million or so circulation, picking out a miscellaneous collection of "funny" jokes which you can, by efforts that would make a contortionist jealous, twist to your purpose. No story should be added to your collection without a careful, challenging examination. Is it explosively funny? Can it be told briefly and adequately within your time limitations? Does it demand a dialect or characterization beyond your limited powers? Is there a sure-fire surprise finish? These are all points to be considered.

Beware especially of that funny story you heard on Eddie Cantor's radio program—or the one somebody told at a banquet the other evening. Remember, other folks get around, too! They've probably heard the story told much better than you are likely to tell it.

If you tell stories particularly well—beware! That is, if you have a serious message to impart. All public men know how fatal a gift of humor may be—unless it is confined by a powerful leash. Once a man gets a reputation for being funny, his effectiveness as a serious speaker is greatly impaired, if not ruined. People *expect* to laugh when they go to hear him, and they will laugh, even at his most serious utterances. Lincoln, a superb story-teller, did not put the slightest hint of humor into his greatest speeches.

But humor, unrestrained, has its place, to be sure. Chauncey Depew was a dignified, and upon occasion even austere, gentleman of great wealth and wide interests. His associates knew him as a keen judge of men and an able executive. But at the proper time and place— as an after-dinner speaker—his wit was unsurpassed.

In another section we are submitting for your consideration a collection of anecdotes, especially selected for your use as a presiding officer. We hope that you may find this small handpicked assortment useful in supplementing your own time-tested collection of good stories.

200 "Break-the-Ice" Anecdotes
—and How to Use Them

In presenting these stories for your consideration, we make no claim that they are the latest, the most original, or the most amusing examples which one may encounter. Candidly, many of these stories have long passed the first blush of youth. They have done faithful service for decades, and perhaps for generations. But let us recall the counsel of that master teller of tales, the late Senator Bob Taylor, of Tennessee. "For solid comfort and general satisfaction," said the Senator, "give me an old, time-worn story. For then the audience is a step ahead of you. They know precisely when and where to laugh."

These stories were selected, let us explain, first and foremost for their practical value to the presiding officer. Each has made the grade here because it seems to us to be the sort of tale one might relate in introducing a speaker, or in adding a trace of gayety to some commonly encountered situation. In some instances, we have suggested a possible application. In other cases, we leave it to your ingenuity to weave the story into the warp and woof of your discourse. We hope that these hand-picked anecdotes may serve you, from time to time, as effectively as they have us.

1—Here is a good story to illustrate the advantages of social contacts, the importance of good fellowship, and the necessity for all of us to work together. Just the thing to use in a campaign for new members or increased attendance:

A certain pastor went to call on a backslider who had once been a regular attendant in his congregation. He found the man sitting beside an open fire. Without saying a word, the minister took the tongs, lifted a glowing coal from the fire and laid it on the hearthstone. In silence they watched it quickly die out. Then the backslider spoke: "You needn't say a word, sir; I'll be there next Sunday!"

+ + +

2—In connection with the reading of the Treasurer's Report (especially if it chances to be a bit depressing) or as a prelude to a campaign for funds, you might well tell this one:

A Methodist minister, invited to speak in an Episcopal church, was asked if he would like a surplice.

"A surplice? Goodness, no!" smiled the genial divine with a merry twinkle. "Remember I am a Methodist preacher. I know nothing of surplices. My only experience has been with deficits."

3—If the mood of the meeting is a merry one, why not express the hope that we may all be actuated by a spirit of gay abandon, such as that which guided the Mama Robin. Each day, when Papa Robin came home from the office, Mama proudly displayed a sky-blue egg, until there in the tidy nest were a total of four. But on the fifth evening, Papa Robin, glancing into the nest prepared to give his usual approbation, met a disturbing spectacle. There lay a white egg, speckled with brown. With a look of mingled anguish and anxiety, he turned a quizzical eye upon his waiting frau. "Oh, that?" she said with assumed nonchalance. "Why I just laid that for a lark."

+   +   +

4—O. Fred Rost, one of the associate editors of *Business Week,* is often introduced by careless presiding officers as the editor of that publication; a situation which used to cause him some embarrassment, until he developed this cannibal story:

It seems that a certain associate editor was shipwrecked and had the misfortune to drift ashore amongst a band of savage cannibals. They captured him and took him into the august presence of the Chief, who was greatly cheered at the prospect of a bit of white meat. "Ah," he said after some extended questioning, "so you are an associate editor. Then you should be of good cheer. A promotion is in store for you. Tomorrow you will be Editor-in-Chief."

+ + +

5—Apropos of doing the best that we can with the materials in hand (a problem that not infrequently confronts the presiding officer) you may well have occasion to tell this tale of little Willie who turned an owl loose in the schoolroom—a distinct violation of the rules and regulations. The Master proceeded to give Willie a warming with a hickory stick. And the next day, Willie's mama came to remonstrate.

"My dear Professor Robbins," she said in accents cultured, "I am quite perturbed by your harsh treatment of William. Don't you think a mother's tears and prayers would have been far more effective than the punishment you inflicted?"

"My dear Madam," replied the sorely-tried prof, "I didn't have any mother's tears, so I used what I had."

+ + +

6—If your speaker has presented an effective talk, well within time limitations, you might extend congratulations and point out that his performance is in marked contrast to that of Mr. Tusher.

Tusher was an orator—in the worst sense of the word. His was the grand manner, with well rounded sentences and plenty of 'em. It is related that once in dedicating a court-house, he began his discourse so far back in ancient history that it took an hour and a half to reach the time of the Caesars. At this point, a town wit audibly whispered to a companion, "Well, thank goodness, we only have to listen to two thousand years more of Tusher's speech."

+ + +

7—If your speaker has confessed that he does not pose as an expert in the subject he proposes to discuss, you might, in acknowledging his modesty, give this definition of an "expert." It is at least a variation of the rather threadbare assertion that "an expert is an ordinary man who happens to be a long way from home":

An expert is defined as a person who crawls slowly and laboriously toward the same goals that you and I reach correctly in one jump—and when he arrives, isn't sure he's there.

+ + +

8—In the flush days of steamboating on the Mississippi, owner-captains attained wealth, power and sometimes more than a little haughtiness. They tell a tale of one such captain, whose finest boat was hailed from a country landing. Veering toward the bank, the mate bellowed the usual, "Whatcha want?"

The ruralite, sitting astride his horse, took a liberal chaw of tobacco and replied, "Want t' speak t' Cap'n Pursell personal." When finally the great man had been summoned, and had stepped out on the hurricane roof, the countryman continued:

"Jest wanted to ask you, Cap'n, kin my hoss have a drink out of yoh river?"

+ + +

9—Emphasizing your point that the Program Committee is lining up some star attractions, you might say frankly that you realize programs must be kept up to par if attendance is to be maintained. Then tell this story of Jack Dionne's:

A tribe of Navajo Indians had for years repulsed every effort of missionaries. They refused to change their religion; wouldn't even come to church to listen to the padre. Finally one came who filled his church every Sunday.

This padre was one who believed in catering to the physical as well as the spiritual man. Every Sunday after services, he gave each member of the flock a plate of hot beans and a cup of coffee.

For months this went on, and he continued to preach to large and attentive audiences. Then one Sunday he found he had neglected to get in his stock of beans. All he was able to give his people was a cup of coffee. The next Sunday only a third of the usual crowd showed up. Once again he gave nothing but coffee.

When he rang the bell on the third Sunday, one lone Navajo appeared. "Where are your people? Why aren't they here?" asked the puzzled padre.

The Navajo was one of those plainspoken men who believe in simple truths directly presented: "My people say, 'No beans—no Jesus'."

+ + +

10—And sometime when *you* have the misfortune to be the speaker, tell this one about the young tender-foot lawyer from the East who adventured into a wild and wooly Western cattle town and hung out his shingle. In the fullness of time he was invited, with some misgivings, to address a Chamber of Commerce meeting. He was scared to death, and showed it by giving a pretty gosh-awful performance. His self-confidence was not restored to any great degree when, at the conclusion of the meeting, three grim-faced cattlemen arose and with a conspicuous display of ropes and guns, made directly for the speaker's table. The young lawyer was all for beating it by a convenient rear exit, but an elder and more experienced head counselled him. "Jest you set still, son. They ain't nobody a-goin' t' harm you. Them fellers is a-comin' fer the Program Chairman!"

11—Here is a story which usually goes over well in a broad-minded mixed audience. I know a few intrepid souls who have told it successfully in talking to groups of women:

A speaker, paying his respects to the fair-sex, pointed out that they were rapidly adventuring into fields once held sacrosanct to the male. "Today," he said impressively, "we have women doctors."

At this point, an inebriated gent in the rear of the hall got laboriously to his feet with a cry of, "Hurrah for wom'n doctorsh!"

Unperturbed, the speaker proceeded, ". . . and women lawyers."

Again the drunk arose, with a cheer for the women lawyers.

"In fact," said the speaker, continuing with grim determination, "today we find that between men and women, there is very little difference."

With a supreme effort the inebriate once more hoisted himself to his feet, with a feeble but earnest cry, "Hurrah for that little difference!"

+ + +

12—If your meeting is late in getting under way, due to the delayed arrival of an important speaker, you might put everyone in a good humor by telling this story of little Johnnie:

Well past the usual supper hour, a neighbor encountered Johnnie playing marbles with some companions of questionable gentility, from the other side of the tracks. "Why, Johnnie," she said reprovingly, "you better hurry on home. You'll be late for supper!"

"Oh, no I won't," said Johnnie, with an air of one who knows his stuff. "I won't be late. I've got the meat!"

+ + +

13—We all admire enterprise and opportunism, and you may find numerous occasions to tell this story of the tramp.

Accosting a gentleman on the streets of St. Louis, this bum varied the usual supplication by making a straightforward confession, "Mister, I need a drink. Will you buy me one?"

Being an admirer of truth, wherever encountered, and likewise an understanding spirit, the man decided to grant the rather unusual request, and concluded that he might as well seize the opportunity to have one himself. So they repaired to a nearby bar, and the gentleman gave the order:

"Two ryes," he said.

"Make mine the same," said the tramp.

+ + +

14—Maybe you'll have a chance sometime to work in this definition: "A Committee is a group that keep minutes and waste hours." And do you remember that definition of a board: Long, wooden, and *thick*.

+ + +

15—Bringing out the point that if you accept responsibility, you should shoulder it manfully, and be prepared for any contingency:

Two gents, somewhat under the influence of liquor, were driving their car on a broad (but not quite broad enough) highway. Suddenly, with a terrific whang they collided with a telephone pole, scattering parts of the car in all directions. "Whatsa matter?" asked Joe of the driver, "Didn't you see that telephone pole?" "Why yes," responded his companion, rubbing his eyes to dispell the fog, "Yes, I seen it all right, but I thought *you* was a-drivin'."

+ + +

16—Stressing the value of determination, in the face of adversity and calamity:

A farmer had an old blind horse which had outlived its usefulness. One day the horse fell into an unused well, and the farmer found him there, standing knee-deep in water. There was no way to get him out, and as both he and the well were useless, the farmer decided to fill the well up, and leave the horse buried in it.

He shoveled the dirt into the well as rapidly as he could. But the horse was not ready to be buried. When the dirt began to pour in upon him, he shook it off and kept treading on the dirt under his feet. Gradually the well filled up, and the horse, at the same time, rose higher and higher, until he was able to step out and walk away to the pasture.

The moral, of course, is that none of us need be buried under hard times, discouragements and calamities, unless we are willing to be buried.

+   +   +

17—If the speaker has dealt with large figures and rather dizzying statistics (as speakers are wont to do in these teeming times) you might in your concluding remarks, tell the story of the simple native who was asked what he would do with a million dollars. "If I had all that money," he pondered, "I'd put $5,000 in the bank, and have a hell of a swell time with the other $5,000."

+   +   +

18—I don't know just where or how you can use it, but at any rate here's one of Bert Lahr's macabre tales, as reported by Mark Hellinger:

A Broadway gunman, it seems, stepped out one night and killed a pal. No sooner had the pal been placed in his grave until his ghost returned to haunt the gunman.

And a most persistent ghost it was. No matter where the gunman went, that ghost was sure to go. The gunman's nerves began to give way. He couldn't eat. He couldn't sleep. His hands began to tremble so that the poor fellow could hardly lift a blackjack. After several weeks of this, he could stand it no longer. He left Broadway and went to California.

But even that failed him. No matter what he did, nothing would make that pesky ghost disappear. He was becoming an absolute wreck. What was he to do? There was only one thing he could do—and he very promptly did it.

He went out and killed another man, in order to get a change of ghosts!

+ + +

19—If your speaker's remarks have been pertinent and pleasing, you might, in thanking him, tell by contrast the story of the Irish section foreman and his celebrated "Cow Report":

A careless bovine, it seems, had come in contact with a train a few miles down the track, and his foreman was called upon to gather up the remains and report thereon. It was his first experience with a rather complicated report, and some of the items were a bit puzzling. But he was a smart lad and used his head. For a time that one on "Disposition of Carcass" had him stumped. But after he had gone around and had another good look at Bossy, he inscribed, without hesitation, "Kind and gentle."

The last item, though, was the real stopper. Our foreman contemplated those challenging dotted lines with mingled feelings of perplexity and disgust. At long last he moistened his stubby indelible pencil and, under the heading of "Remarks" wrote: "She didn't make none. She was dead."

+　+　+

20—Sooner or later you will have occasion to introduce a lawyer. For lawyers are incorrigible public speakers. If he is a good fellow, able to take a joke at the expense of his profession (and most legal lights are pretty well hardened by this time) you might try out this one:

The young lawyer's wife was fretting over the bareness of their home. "We need furniture, drapes, carpets—everything," she wailed. "Cheer up, my dear," comforted her spouse. "I have an excellent divorce case now pending. I represent the wife, and the husband has plenty of money. As soon as I finish breaking up their home, we can fix ours up."

+　+　+

21—This one concerns an experience of a Sunday School teacher in an eastern Pennsylvania town, where most of the population is made up of railway employees.

For a couple of weeks before Christmas, he had tried to impress upon his class the story of Bethlehem. On the third Sunday he asked:

"And where was Jesus born?"

"Mauch Chunk," answered one bright lad promptly.

"Why no!" answered the teacher, horror stricken. "The very idea! Jesus was born in Bethlehem."

"Oh, yes," responded the lad, "I knew it was some place on the Lehigh Valley Railroad."

+ + +

21A—If your guest has a reputation as a particularly engaging and convincing speaker, you might, in introducing him, tell the story of the prisoner who was called into the warden's office.

"You were sent here, I believe," said the warden, "for writing a glowing prospectus for an oil company."

"Yes," said the prisoner, "I guess I was a little too optimistic."

"Ah," said the warden thoughtfully, "By the way, the governor wants a report on conditions in this prison. I was thinking that perhaps I might prevail upon you to write it."

+ + +

22—When your program includes a singer who forsakes the classical and renders popular ballads in a popular way, try this story in expressing your appreciation:

Asked for a definition of classical music, one of our townsmen replied:

"Well, when a piece threatens every minute to be a tune and always disappoints you, it's classical."

+ + +

23—Sometime you might be able to use this revealing definition of a convention:

A convention is what hotels put back their revolving doors after.

+ + +

24—A rookie, lately arrived at an army training camp was curiously inspecting the live stock at too close range when one of the mules kicked him cold. His buddies got him on the rebound, placed him on a stretcher and started for the infirmary. Regaining consciousness, the rookie felt the swaying motion of the stretcher, and cautiously lowering his hands over the side, found only space.

"Gosh!" he moaned in horror, "I ain't hit ground yet!"

+ + +

25—One of these days you'll run into a situation where, for one reason or another, you may find it expedient not to take sides. This story may give you a good out, or at least fill the gap while you stall for time to collect your thoughts. Every presiding officer should have at least one such tale in his collection. They are an ever-present help in time of trouble:

The candidate for public office, in the midst of a campaign speech was finding it rather tough going. Pausing for a moment to collect his thoughts, a prompter whispered, "Talk about the tariff."

"Ah, yes," said the candidate brightening. "And now, about the tariff. . . . There's a question we've had with us for years. Some want a low tariff, and there are others who demand a high tariff. And after giving the subject careful thought, so far as I am concerned, so do I."

+ + +

26—"I understand," said the questioner, "that Mr. Smithers who was with your firm was a tried and trusted employee."

The banker looked at the visitor coldly. "Ah, yes," he said reminiscently, "he was trusted—and he will be tried, if we're fortunate enough to catch him."

+ + +

27—A census-taker, working in the deep south, encountered a negro mammy bending over a wash-tub.

Explaining his mission he asked, "How many children have you?"

"Weel-l, now, lemmee ree-collec'. There's David, an' Jonah, an' Joshuay, an' Ruth, an' Jezebell, an' . . ."

"Now, Mammy," interrupted the government agent, "I don't care about the details. Just give me the number."

"Numbah? Lawdy, Mistah, we hasn't started that. Why, we ain't nigh out o' names yit!"

+ + +

28—A Scotch farmer had gone with his wife to an aviation field, where they tentatively considered a trip aloft. But the price was far too steep.

"Ten dullers!" stormed the Scot, "why 'tis an outrage! A duller a minute! I'll pay no such."

But the aviator, sensing an opportunity for a bit of fun, determined to make a counter proposition. "I'll tell you what I'll do," he suggested, "since you're so eager for a trip, I'll take you and your wife for nothing, if you'll agree not to say a word all the time you're in the air. But if you say anything while you're up there, it's going to cost you the full price. Is that agreeable to you?"

The pair considered briefly, and then agreed.

So in they climbed. When the plane had reached an altitude of 3,000 feet, the aviator began his effort to make the Scot shout. He went into loops, tail spins, the barrel roll—everything. But not a word was heard from the passengers. Finally, disgusted and defeated, the pilot returned to the ground.

"Well," he said, with forced admiration, "I must say I've got to hand it to you. Any other novice would have been hollering at the top of his lungs. You've certainly got pluck."

"Ah, weel," said the canny Scot deprecatingly, "ye almos' had me there once, when the old lady fell out!"

+ + +

29—If the speaker has woven some tall tales into his discourse, you might retaliate with this one:

"It was my first grizzly," said the Western guide, giving his customary recital to a group of tenderfeet, "so I was mighty proud to kill him in a hand-to-hand struggle. We started to fight about sunrise. When he finally gave up the ghost, the sun was going down."

At this point the guide paused impressively to note the effect of his story. Not a word was said, so the narrator added very slowly, *"for the second time."*

"I gather, then," remarked one of the group, "that it required a period of two days to enable you to dispose of that grizzly."

"Two days and a night," said the guide solemnly. "That grizzly died mighty hard."

"Choked to death?" asked the Easterner.

"Yes, *sir!*" answered the guide promptly.

"Pardon me," continued the tourist, "but what did you try to get *him* to swallow?"

30—If your program is unavoidably delayed in getting under way, you might quiet a restless audience with this one of the bachelor, notorious for his slowness. He had, it seems, been courting a maiden for two years without coming to the point. Finally the father decided to take a hand.

"Clinton," he began on the swain's next visit. "Clinton, you've been settin' up with Nellie, an' takin' her to picnics, and to church and sech for a mighty long time now, and nothin's come of it. So now, Clinton, I'm a'askin' you man to man, what is your intentions?"

"Well, now, sir," said the bachelor quite unabashed, "answerin' you man to man, I'd say there ain't no cause fer you to get all concerned. My intentions, sir, is honorable—honorable, but remote."

+ + +

31—Another tall tale you may be able to use sometime:

An Englishman and an American, in London, were arguing concerning the muddy thoroughfares.

"True," said the Englishman, "some of our streets are a trifle greasy at this season, but nothing to be concerned about."

"Well," said the American, "you may think differently when I tell you of my adventure."

"Indeed?" replied the Londoner, "and what was that?"

"Well, this very afternoon, I was walking along, impressed of course by the fact that the mud was very thick and deep. Presently, I observed a high hat afloat on a large puddle of very rich ooze. Thinking to do someone a kindness, I gave the hat a poke with my stick, when an old gentleman looked up from beneath, surprised and frowning.

"Hello!" I said, "You're in pretty deep!"

" 'Deeper than you think,' he said, 'I'm standing on top of an omnibus!' "

+ + +

32—A northern tourist, motoring through one of the most desolate regions of Arkansas, observed a native working industriously in a field. This impressed him as rather a novelty in that section where everyone seemed averse to labor. So he hailed the native.

"My friend," he said, "you look like a live chap and a hustler."

"Well, I aim to keep busy."

"That's what I said to myself as I saw you. I'm wondering why you are content to slave your life out in this God-forsaken country. I never saw such poor looking soil in my life. Why don't you pull up stakes and move up into Ohio where I live?"

The hillsman shook his head.

"You see, stranger, I've always lived hereabouts, and I reckon I'll stay awhile longer."

"Well," said the tourist, "every man to his own fancy. I guess a fellow might get attached even to such a spot as this. But what can you expect by staying on? You're bound to get poorer and poorer all the time."

"Mister," said the hillsman earnestly, "I'm a blame sight better off than you 'pear to think. Why I don't own nary acre of this here land."

+ + +

33—There are times when patience ceases to be a virtue. If you have occasion to stir a lethargic group into action, try this little character sketch:

All his life misfortune had dogged his steps, yet never once was he heard to complain. He got married, and his wife ran away with the hired man. He had a daughter, and the daughter was deceived by a villain of deepest dye. He had a son, and the son was lynched. A fire burnt his barn; a cyclone blew away his home; a hailstorm destroyed his crops; the banker foreclosed the mortgage, taking his farm. Yet at each fresh stroke of misfortune, his patience seemed inexhaustible.

After a time, penniless but still submissive, he landed in the county poorhouse. One day the overseer sent him out to plough a potato field. A thunderstorm came up, but was passing over when, without warning, a bolt of lightning descended. It melted the ploughshare, stripped off most of the man's clothing, singed his beard, branded his naked back with the initials of a neighboring cattleman, and hurled the startled victim through a barbed wire fence.

When he regained consciousness, he got slowly to his knees, clasped his hands and raised his eyes toward heaven. Then for the first time he asserted himself.

"Lord," he said, "this here is gettin' to be plumb ridiculous!"

+   +   +

34—Here's another dandy introductory story, for an occasion when you are so unfortunate as to be the Speaker of the Day:

Mark Twain, in making an after-dinner speech, once said:

"Speaking of fresh eggs, I am reminded of the town of Squash. In my early lecturing days, I went to Squash to lecture in the Temperance Hall, arriving in the afternoon. The town seemed very poorly billed. I thought I'd find out if the people knew anything at all about what was in store for them. So I turned in at the general store.

" 'Good afternoon, friend,' I said to the general storekeeper, 'Any entertainment here tonight to help a stranger while away his evening?'

"The storekeeper, who was sorting mackerel, straightened up, wiped his briny hands on his apron, and said:

" 'I expect there's goin' to be a lecture. I been sellin' eggs all day.' "

+   +   +

35—The next time you have occasion to discuss chiseling (and most of us do now and again) you might trot out this story of the two Jewish gentlemen:

"Now, I'm telling you, Abie, there's a real suit of clothes! The material you can't beat it. The style is right up to tomorrow, and it fits you like nobody's business. An eighty dollar suit of clothes, Abie, but I'm not charging you that; nor seventy dollars, nor even sixty dollars yet. I'll tell you, Abie, what I'll do; I'm making you that suit at fifty dollars flat!"

"Well, Jake, I'm liking the suit okay, but I'll not pay you fifty dollars for it; nor forty dollars either; no, nor not even thirty dollars. I'm paying you twenty-five dollars for this suit, Jake, and you should take it or leave it."

"Sold! That's the way I like to do business, Abie; no chiseling."

+   +   +

36—There's such a thing, you know, as having so much system, theory and red tape that you never get anything done. When you run up against such a situation, here's a useful story:

A railway bridge had been destroyed by fire, and it was necessary to rebuild it. The bridge engineer and his staff were urged to immediate action. A couple of days later, the superintendent of the division visited the scene and encountered an old master bridge builder.

"Bill," said the superintendent, "I want this job rushed. Every hour's delay is costing the company money. Have you got the engineer's plans for the new bridge?"

"I don't know," said the bridge builder, "whether the engineer has the picture drawed yet or not, but the bridge is up and the trains is passin' over it."

✦ ✦ ✦

37—A farmer lad who had been sent to a woodland pasture to fetch the cows returned to report that he couldn't find them.

"That's strange," commented the farmer. "Where did you look?"

"I looked everywhere."

"Now see here, son, the cows are bound to be there. Tell me just where you went to look for them."

"Well, I went up there to the end of the lane, and then I—I just scattered."

And that, someone has observed, is about the way some speakers discuss a subject!

38—Bishop Foss once visited a Philadelphia physician, and in the course of an examination was asked, "Do you talk in your sleep?"

"No," smiled the bishop, "I talk in other people's sleep."

+ + +

39—You'll never have too many stories on the theme of ACTION. Here's another for your collection:

A pastor received a "call" from a larger church. It was a better and more remunerative pastorate. He re-plied that he would prayerfully consider the matter and give his decision in a few days. A short time later, the pastor's son was asked if his father had decided to accept the offer. "I don't know," he replied, "papa is still pray-ing, but mama has the things nearly all packed."

+ + +

40—They had been watching the high diver who ac-companied the street carnival. The official village liar held out as long as he could, but finally spoke:

"Well, that was purty good, all right; but I had a cousin once who could beat him."

Prodded by the onlookers for more particulars, he proceeded: "Well, this cousin o' mine was the champeen high diver of the world—that's all."

"What did he ever do to win that title?" someone asked.

"Well, he done considerable in the divin' line, which was his specialty. I recollect once he made a bet of a hundred dollars that he could dive from Liverpool, England to New York City."

The skeptic gave a groan of resignation.

"I suppose you're goin' to ask us to believe that he won that there bet."

"No," answered the liar a bit sorrowfully. "No, I hain't. I hain't a-goin' to lie to you. That there was one o' the few bets my cousin ever lost. Somehow he jest miscalculated his distance. He come up in Denver, Colorado!"

✦ ✦ ✦

41—This ingenious explanation of the tangled finances of a Negro lodge might well serve in many a situation. You can use it—and how!

"De committee on finances ob dis heah lodge will now make a repo't," announced the chairman.

The spokesman arose, cleared his throat impressively, and announced: "De committee on finances, aftah considerin' into de financial an' peculiary affairs ob dis lodge, has discobered what am de trouble wid dem peculiary affairs what is keepin' de treasury so low. We begs to repo't dat de chief cause of de finances bein' so low is all caused by de lack ob money."

42—You are doggoned lucky if you do not occasionally have to report to your membership that some enterprise or other is not progressing as rapidly as you had hoped. In such cases, point out that all things worthwhile take time—and tell them this story:

A Hebrew tailor had been commissioned to make a pair of trousers. The customer called several times only to be informed that the tailor had not yet had an "inspiration" for the pants, but would get at the assignment presently.

Finally the creation was completed, and the customer was satisfied.

"Yes, it's a good job, Goldblatt," he agreed grudgingly, "but it took you too infernally long. Why the Lord made the world in six days—and it took you a month to turn out a pair of pants!"

Goldblatt continued to eye his handiwork with undisguised admiration. "Vell, that is maybe so," he responded, "but I'm telling you, Mister, take a look at the world—and then take another look at those pants!"

+ + +

43—If you're stuck with a rather long and involved explanation—and feel your inadequacy to present the situation to your audience—you'll search a long time for a better story than this one to "break the ice":

One day last winter a long, lanky Florida cracker drifted into a life-saving station on the Southern coast, and applied for a job as guard. He was perhaps the tallest individual ever encountered in those parts—close onto seven feet—and a rather likely looking chap, so they put him through the usual quiz. And finally, just as a matter of form, they asked if he could swim.

"Well, no," the boy confessed reluctantly, "I can't swim to do no good, but"—and he looked down at those long, gangling legs—"but I can wade to beat hell!"

You might then add that if you can't get along swimingly with the subject assigned to you, you will at least wade right in.

+ + +

44—When, as a speaker, you are called upon to play a "return engagement" you may find this story helpful, in expressing your surprise at so large a gathering, or in explanation of a rather meager turn-out, as the case may be:

When Maurice Francis Eagan was United States Minister at Copenhagen he made a practice of going through the provinces of Denmark once a year and lecturing on American literature.

One night when the present King of Denmark was dining at the United States Legation, the King, who was at that time Crown Prince, said to Mr. Eagan:

"I receive agreeable reports of your lectures in the provinces. Do you use a different lecture every time?"

"I always use the same one, Your Majesty," the minister answered.

"But what do you do if people come a second time?"

"They never come a second time," was the answer.

+ + +

45—Two elderly women were talking, and one said:

"I am entertaining two locust preachers in my home."

The other laughed. "That was a funny slip; you meant local of course, dear."

"No, I said locust and I *meant* locust."

"But locusts—why locusts are things that come in swarms, and eat everything in sight, and—"

"Don't I know it!" snapped her friend, "and I'm entertaining two of 'em in my home this week!"

+ + +

46—Here is a story suitable for any professional gathering where the rewards of the profession are spiritual and mental rather than monetary:

I have just learned of an editor (teacher, doctor, scientist, or what have you) who started poor at the age of twenty, and retired with a comfortable fortune of $50,000. This was acquired through industry, economy, conscientious effort, perseverance, and the death of an uncle who left him $49,990.

47—We have listened to speeches where this story would seem to be very appropriate. Maybe you have, too:

An American on a trip to China was asked to speak before a Chinese audience. He accepted the invitation. During the course of his talk, he noticed that a Chinese in a corner of the room was writing on a blackboard. He became interested and as he spoke, watched the man who was writing in Chinese. The writer wrote less and finally stopped completely.

When he had finished speaking, the American asked the chairman of the meeting what this man had been doing.

"Why," said the chairman, "he was interpreting your speech for the benefit of the members who do not understand English."

"But," said the speaker, "for the last twenty minutes he did not put down anything."

"Oh," the chairman said smoothly, "he was only writing the *ideas* on the blackboard."

+ + +

48—If a speaker has taken rather less time than anticipated, compliment him on getting across a message in a few words. Then, if you're running a bit ahead of schedule, you might fill in with this one:

A wealthy self-made man—and not too well made at that—decided he would have his portrait painted. He approached a well-known artist and inquired his terms, and the length of time it would take him. The artist said he would undertake the commission for $500, and estimated that it would take about two weeks. He was given the job.

The work went rather better than the artist had expected, and he was able to finish the portrait in ten days. He informed his client that it was finished. The self-made man exploded:

"Here you promise me two weeks' work for $500, and you've worked only ten days. I won't pay! Either you work four days more, or the deal is off!"

The artist obligingly assented. He spent the next four days lengthening the ears of his patron.

+ + +

49—This is a very old one, but still far too good to discard:

The minister had a reputation for being long-winded, and on this occasion was in prime condition. For more than an hour he had droned along on his text, the Prophets of the Bible.

"Now then," he said at long last, "we have disposed of the Major Prophets. Next we come to the Minor Prophets. To what place shall we assign the Minor Prophets?"

"Well, parson," came a tired voice from the congregation, "one of 'em can have my place, I'm going home."

50—They say this one really happened, over in the region of the TVA operations, in Tennessee:

Down a steep, twisting grade came a ten-ton government truck loaded with dynamite. At the wheel sat a mountain youngster, a raw recruit. As he guided the dangerous cargo over the treacherous path, the boy puffed unconcernedly at a half-smoked cigarette.

From a temporary shack office a straw-boss looked up. At one quick glance he took in truck, dynamite and the live cigarette. He sprang to his feet yelling, and frantically waving his arms as he raced in the direction of the truck.

"Throw that cigarette away, you xx!! &&!! Throw it *away!*"

Slowly, methodically, the mountain boy applied the brakes, brought his craft to a groaning, screeching halt, and finally, removing the cigarette from his lips, deposited it by the wayside.

When at last he could spare the breath, the boss expostulated: "You idiot! You lunatic! You lunkhead! Don't you know better than to smoke a cigarette when you're haulin' *dynamite?* Don't you know a spark is likely to set off ten tons o' that stuff and blow this whole countryside to smithereens?"

The boy was frankly impressed, but bewildered. Slowly, he turned his puzzled blue eyes upon the excited speaker. A wrinkle of earnest reflection was furrowed on his brow, as he drawled, "Well, Mister, it ain't *been* a-doin' it!"

+   +   +

51—The uses you'll find for this one!

Over in a little hamlet in Illinois there is a man who has the agency for a popular car in the low-price field. And on a population quota basis, he sells more cars than any other dealer in the territory. A zone manager determined to find out why and how the record was maintained. After spending a day or so with the dealer he was still puzzled. The man seemed to possess no evident genius. He was uneducated; in fact almost illiterate. Nor was he noticeably more aggressive than any number of other representatives. Finally, the perplexed zone manager asked the agent frankly for the secret of his sales record.

Secretly flattered, the small-town man gave the question thoughtful consideration. Obviously he was expected to say something profoundly important. But for the life of him he couldn't think of a thing.

"I ain't rightly got no secret, I reckon," he finally confessed. "Mostly I look around for a likely prospect, and then I jest *constipate* on him."

+   +   +

52—The hecklers were many and active, but the lecturer lectured on. He was undaunted, although he certainly found it hard going.

Finally, however, he halted, gazed patiently around the hall, and cleared his throat.

"I'll just digress for a second," he said, "to inform the persons who are interrupting me that instead of confusing me, they succeed only in egging me on."

Then a voice suggested:

"Well, if that's so, it's about time they changed tactics and started egging you off."

+ + +

53—To emphasize the point that an organization does not grow in numbers or influence, without some concentrated effort:

The Sunday-School teacher had been telling the story of Spring, and the miracle of the growth of the Easter lily.

"Now, children," she said, "who can tell me what it is that makes the lily spring from this little bulb?"

"God does it," replied one little lad who had learned his lesson well, "but fertilizer helps some."

+ + +

54—The soldiers marched to the church and halted in the square outside. One wing of the edifice was undergoing repairs, so there was room for only about half the group.

"Sergeant," ordered the captain, "tell the men who don't want to go to church to fall out."

A large number quickly availed themselves of the privilege.

"Now, sergeant," said the captain, "dismiss all the men who did not fall out and march the others in—they need it most."

+ + +

55—Another proof of the effectiveness of brevity:

It was the period reserved for English composition, and the teacher had suggested as a theme, Baseball. Each pupil was to write an account of a ball game. All fell earnestly to work, with the exception of a single lad who chewed reluctantly at his pen. Finally his countenance was illuminated by a Great Inspiration. Turning to the blank sheet before him, he wrote:

"Rain—no game."

+ + +

56—Certainly there should be no need to point out the moral—or the application—of this one:

A visitor at an insane asylum noted the patients sitting about with only an occasional guard to keep an eye on them.

"Aren't you afraid," he asked one of the girl attendants, "that these inmates may become violent and do you bodily injury?"

"Not in the least."

"But suppose," persisted the visitor, "suppose they should organize and attack you, what would you do?"

"Organize!" snapped the girl contemptuously. "If they had sense enough to organize, do you suppose they would be here?"

+   +   +

57—Time and again you've heard that old "Rat-and-Cat-Farm" gag, but maybe you'd like to have an authentic version for the record. So here it is:

A cat ranch is now being organized with 100,000 cats. Each cat will average 12 kittens a year. The cat skins will sell for thirty cents each. One hundred men can skin 5,000 cats a day. We figure a daily profit of over $10,000.

What shall we feed the cats?

We will start a rat ranch next door with 1,000,000 rats. The rats will breed twelve times faster than the cats. So we'll have four rats to feed each day to every cat. Now, what shall we feed the rats? We will feed the rats the carcasses of the cats, after they have been skinned.

Now Get This

We feed the rats to the cats, and the cats to the rats, and get the catskins for nothing. Shares in this enterprise are selling rapidly, but the price will soon advance. Get in on the ground floor. Invest now!

58—If this isn't a new high in diplomacy and quick-on-the-trigger thinking, then we'd certainly like to hear your entry:

A clergyman noticed a woman whom he very much disliked coming up his front steps. Taking refuge in his study, he left his wife to entertain the caller. Half an hour later he emerged from his retreat, listened carefully at the landing, and hearing nothing below, called to his wife, "Has that old pest gone?" Well, it turned out that she hadn't! But the minister's wife was equal to the occasion: "Yes, dear," she replied, "she went long ago! Mrs. Parker is here now."

+ + +

59—And they do say that knocking, in an individual, is just as much an evidence of lack of power as it is in an automobile.

+ + +

60—"Ah wants a conjunction agin' my wife," announced the colored supplicant at the bar of justice. "She done th'oed me clean out o' a secon'-story window, right spang on a pile ob bricks."

"Well, Sam," said the judge, "you don't seem to be any worse for the fall. Not hurt, are you?"

"No, sah, Ah ain' hurt, but s'posin' she does it agin an' dem bricks ain' there?"

61—Pat and Mike had been fishing with excellent results.

"We'll come again tomorrer," Mike suggested, "and, Pat, we must hit this vury same shpot. Shure and there's no place like it."

"That's right," Pat agreed, "but howiver can we know the vury place again?"

"Oi'll fix that," exclaimed Mike. "Here we are!"

He leaned carefully over, before they pulled up the anchor and, taking a bit of chalk from his pocket, he made a big cross on the side of the boat.

"There!" he cried exultantly, "that settles it!"

Pat scratched his head.

"But how do we know," he asked, "that we'll get the same boat tomorrer?"

+ + +

62—Most of us, probably, have been tempted in a manner like unto that of the old lady whose experience is here related:

A dignified old lady, ascending the steps of the church, encountered some difficulty and asked a gentleman to assist her. Upon reaching the door of the church she thanked him and asked, "Do you happen to know who is preaching this morning?"

"The rector, madam," she was told.

"Oh," she said, "then might I beg you to do me another favor?"

"Certainly," replied the gentleman (who it chanced was none other than the rector himself), "what can I do for you?"

"Would you," asked the old lady, "be good enough to assist me down the steps again?"

+   +   +

63—Here is a story that, more than once, has proved effective in maintaining order:

A clergyman paused in the midst of his discourse to eye a group of disturbers with evident disapproval. "I am always reluctant to expose those who misbehave during services," he said at length, "because of an experience I had some years ago. A young man who sat before me was laughing, talking and making grimaces. I was annoyed and rebuked him severely. Later I was told that I had made a grave mistake. The man I had reproved was an idiot."

During the remainder of the service there was good order.

+   +   +

64—And there is the case of the earnest young clergyman whose congregations were so small that when, during the evening service, he said "Dearly Beloved" the young ladies all felt that they were receiving a proposal.

65—"Breddren," confessed deacon Elijah Snow, "Ah come mouty nigh backslidin' las' Sadday night. De tempter come to me an' led mah sinful feet to Mistah Johnsing's turkey-coop.

"Ah done mah best t' resis', but all de time mah conscience say 'Stop,' de tempter he say 'Go on!'—an' Ah kep gettin' closer an' closer.

"But praise de Lawd! Jes' when Ah was a-goin' t' climb dat fence and make fo' de coop, my ol' houn' dawg treed a possum in Mistah Johnsing's wood-lot, an' de back-slide leave me in a minute!

"An' befo' Ah get up dat tree, de moon come out f'um behin' a cloud and dar stood Mistah Johnsing behin' dat coop, wid a shotgun in his han'.

"Yassah! Ah call out t' Mistah Johnsing to come shoot dat possum mah dog done treed; an' Ah wants t' say dey was a most powahful load o' buckshot in dat gun!

"An' dat's why Ah say that when de tempter come to us, an' show us wheah at dar's a turkey-coop, we oughter rejoice dat Providence is done give us a houn' dawg, an' done give a possum appetite to de black man."

+ + +

66—Harry Lauder's version of the old "1-just-came-for-the-ride" gag:

At a funeral in Glasgow, a well-dressed stranger took a seat in one of the mourning coaches.

The other occupants, curious, struck up a conversation:

"Ye'll be a brither o' the corp?"

"No; I'm no brither o' the corp."

"Weel, ye'll be his cousin?"

"No; I'm no' his cousin."

"At any rate, ye'll be a frien' o' the corp?"

"No; I'm no' that, either. Ye see, I've no' been very weel mysel', an my doctor ordered me carriage exercise, so I thocht this would be the cheapest way to tak' it."

67—A useful example of enterprise:

You may recall the prophecy made, some years ago, that at a specified hour on a certain date, an earthquake was destined to rip open the heart of the city of Chicago. As the hour approached, a crowd of the mildly or morbidly curious had gathered for signs of the first tremor.

While the crowd waited, keyed for impending disaster, a Jewish lad was observed making his way from group to group: "Earthqueck in five minutes! Get your obera glesses and eskimo pies now!"

+ + +

68—And by contrast to the foregoing, there is the story of the two Negro push-cart operators:

At a Presidential inauguration in Washington some years ago, as dense crowds packed the sidewalks, preceding the inaugural parade, a Negro with a push-cart made his way crying lustily, "Popcorn! Peanuts! Candy! Chewing gum!" And a short distance behind him, with shiftless, lazy tread plodded a second and very listless vendor, mumbling, "Same here; same here."

+ + +

69—A Hebrew, driving a small cart drawn by a donkey, came to a toll bridge.

After a heated argument, the Hebrew paid the small fee and went on his way. In the afternoon he returned, but this time he had the donkey seated in the vehicle, and he himself was dragging the cart.

"Here!" said the attendant, stopping him, "you know you've got to pay a toll to cross this bridge."

The Hebrew shook his head and pointed to the donkey. "You shouldn't talk vit me. Esk de driver."

+ + +

70—"Father," said the minister's son, "my teacher says that 'collect' and 'congregate' mean the same thing."

"Perhaps they do, my son, but you may tell your teacher that there is a great deal of difference between a congregation and a collection."

+ + +

71—Henry Ward Beecher, contemplating the purchase of a horse, was examining an animal that had been offered to him. "Mr. Beecher," said the owner, "there's a remarkably fine horse. He will work in any place you put him; never balks or displays his temper, and he can do all that any horse can do."

"Ah," said Beecher, a bit wistfully, "I wish to goodness he was a member of my congregation!"

+ + +

72—A boy with rather mediocre talents was anxious to become a public speaker. "Do you think," he asked his instructor, "that if I were to fill my mouth with pebbles and practice enunciation, as did Demosthenes of old, that it would improve my delivery?"

"Well," said the candid instructor, "if what I have heard is a fair sample, I would suggest that you use Portland cement."

+ + +

73—This is an old one (you might say to your audience) but I am going to tell it anyway. You know, a story in the system is like murder—it will out. Nothing you can say will dissuade the earnest story-teller. Try it sometime. If he asks, "Have you heard this one?" answer, "Frequently." He may look abashed for a moment, but it's ten to one he'll go right ahead and tell the story anyway.

74—Fred Kelly tells this story of his uncle's experience in trapping wild turkeys. The trap was a large box affair supported by a pole. A cord tied to the pole extended to the bushes, where Fred's uncle was hiding.

"One day," he says, "while Uncle waited, a flock of twelve turkeys approached. Eleven of them walked inside the trap.

" 'Just a minute,' Uncle said to himself, 'I'll have the other one.'

"But while he waited, three of the eleven walked out. Cursing his luck, Uncle reflected that as soon as one of the three went back in, he would pull the cord. But five more walked out. That left only three inside; but there was still plenty of corn in the trap, so he continued to wait. But two more soon departed, leaving a single turkey in the trap. While Uncle was trying to decide what to do, the one remaining turkey decided to join his companions—and the trap was empty."

+ + +

75—There are, you know, only two kinds of conversationalists: those who listen to what the other person has to say, and those who use the interval, while someone else is speaking to plan their next remark.

+ + +

76—Mark Twain once remarked that, while it may be unfair, the simple truth is that the more enjoyment you get out of your work, the greater your financial reward is likely to be.

+ + +

77—"Passing the buck" is perhaps our most common pastime. An English justice once observed that the greater part of his judicial time was spent in looking into collisions between motorcars, each on its own side of the road, each sounding its horn, and each stationary.

+ + +

78—"Mistah Baker," an old Negro retainer said to his employer, "will you-all please sah buy me a gallon o' gin, when you goes t' town, an' deduc' it from the monies Ah got comin' t' me Sadday?"

The white man agreed, but when he returned, not seeing the old man, he gave the gin to one of the Negro's nephews to deliver. Later, when he met the old man, he explained what he had done.

"Um-m-m," said the darkey despondently. "No wondah Ah ain' got de gin! Mistah Baker, you-all might jest as well try t' sen' lettuce by a rabbit!"

+ + +

79—Mozart was once asked by a young man for advice on the best way to go about writing a symphony. Not wishing to be discourteous or discouraging, the composer suggested tactfully. "You are quite young. Why not begin with a simpler form—ballads?"

"But," persisted the young man, "you composed symphonies when you were ten years old."

"Yes," answered Mozart, "but I didn't ask 'how'."

+ + +

80—A tramp once had the misfortune to pause at the door of an elderly woman who was very conscientious, and rather lacking in the quality of mercy. He asked for something to eat, and the woman returned presently with a single slice of bread.

"My man," she said, handing him the bread, "I do not believe in idleness of any kind. The devil finds work for idle hands to do. But I am giving you this bread in the name of God, from whom all blessings flow."

The tramp looked at the bread and said thoughtfully,

"Well, for Christ's sake, lady, can't you put some butter on it?"

+ + +

81—It was a pleasant Sunday afternoon, and the old German had taken his young son to a nearby tavern. The father had partaken rather liberally of beer, but decided nevertheless that this would be a good time to warn his son against the evils of intemperance.

"Never drink too much, my boy. To be drunk is a disgrace."

"Yes, Father, but how shall I tell when I have had enough to drink?"

The old man pointed with his finger.

"Do you see those two men sitting in the corner? If you should see four men there, you would know that you were drunk."

"Yes, Father, but—but there is only one man in that corner."

+ + +

82—A noted jurist had attended Sunday services. Asked for a comment on the sermon, he replied that it was like the peace and mercy of God. "Yes," he continued, amplifying his statement, "it was like the peace of God because it passed all understanding, and like His mercy, I thought it would have endured forever."

+ + +

83—The minister, addressing a Sunday School class had taken for his theme the story of Elisha on his journey to Bethel—how the youngsters had taunted the old prophet, and how they were punished when two bears came out of the wild and ate forty and two of them.

"And now, children," concluded the pastor, wishing to stress the moral point, "what does this story show?"

"It shows," ventured one little girl timidly, "how many children two bears can hold."

+ + +

84—And still another, dealing with the ministry, and the ever-popular theme of brevity:

A minister greatly surprised his congregation by delivering a sermon of but ten minutes' duration.

Upon the conclusion of his remarks, he explained:

"I regret to inform you, brethren, that my dog, who appears to be inordinately fond of paper, this morning ate that portion of my sermon which I have not delivered. Let us pray."

At the conclusion of the services, the clergyman was approached by a stranger from another parish. "Doctor," he said, "I would like to know whether that dog of yours has any pups. If it has, I want to get one for my minister."

✛ ✛ ✛

85—Here's one you might use in introducing a specialist:

The young man of a family was asked the name of the family doctor. "Well," he answered, "I hardly know. Mother goes to an eye specialist; father to a stomach specialist; my sister goes to a throat specialist; my brother is in the care of a lung specialist, and right now I'm taking some treatments from an osteopath."

✛ ✛ ✛

86—A husky young man, charged with assault and battery, stoutly maintained that he had merely pushed the plaintiff "a little bit."

The prosecutor insisted upon a more specific testimony. "Well, about how hard?"

"Oh, just a little bit," repeated the defendant.

"Now," said the exasperated attorney, "for the benefit of the judge and jury, please step down here and with me for the subject, illustrate how hard you mean."

Realizing that the witness was in a rather trying position, the prosecutor thought the young man would perhaps overdo the matter to get back at him, and thus incriminate himself.

The defendant promptly descended, approached the attorney, slapped him in the face, kicked him on the shins, seized him bodily, and finally with a great display of strength, lifted the surprised individual from the floor and threw him across a table.

Then facing the court he explained gently:

"Your honor, and gentlemen, about one-tenth that hard."

+ + +

87—In a self-deprecatory mood, this one may have its uses:

An Indian named Big Smoke served as a missionary in his tribe. Once asked what he did for a living, the Indian replied:

"Umph! Me preach."

"That so? What do you get for preaching?"

"Get ten dollar a year."

"Well, that's damned poor pay."

"Umph! Me damned poor preacher."

+ + +

88—A little girl had listened intently to the sermon which dealt with the separation of the sheep and goats. That night, after she had gone to bed, she was heard sobbing.

"It's those goats I'm thinking about," she told her perturbed mother. "I—I'm dreadfully afraid I'm a goat, so I'll never go to heaven. Oh, I'm so afraid I'm a goat!"

Mother quieted and reassured her weeping child, but the following night Jenny was heard weeping again, and again she explained:

"I'm afraid about the goats."

"But mother has told you that you are a little lamb, and that you must never worry about being a goat."

But this time Jenny was not so easily comforted.

"Yes, mama, I know that," she declared softly, "I know that. But I'm afraid—awful afraid you're a goat!"

+ + +

89—It is possible, perhaps, to overdo even such excellent virtues as efficiency and economy. An efficiency man retained by one of the big motor companies in the low priced field developed what he thought was a lulu of an idea. After all, why should we build doors on *both* sides of a motor car? He figured out that an important piece of money could be saved if doors on all models were swung on the left side only. Bubbling over with enthusiasm for his idea, he took it to a conference of top-drawer executives. When he had outlined his plan, the motor moguls were stunned for a moment, then one hardened engineer spoke:

"That's all right," he said, "but you don't go far enough. I suggest we build cars with no openings, give the customer a can-opener, and let him cut the blankety-blank door wherever he pleases!"

+ + +

90—The penitent sinner was impressed by the eloquence of the evangelist—but still had an eye to practical considerations.

"Friends," he said, "I want to repent and tell how bad I have been, but I dasn't do it while the grand jury is in session."

"The Lord will forgive!" shouted the revivalist.

"Yes, but He ain't on that grand jury!"

+ + +

91—As most literate persons must know, Dr. Nicholas Murray Butler, President of Columbia University, is not precisely averse to making public appearances. This fact gives point to Clarence Buddington Kelland's introduction of the good Doctor, at a session of the Dutch Treat Club. "For years," he said, beaming upon Dr. Butler, "organizations have been besieging this retiring gentleman to address them—with remarkable success."

As Jack Goodman, who tells this story, points out, much of the success of such a subtle crack depends upon the delivery. Point those last three words by too much inflection, and the remark becomes only mildly funny. Don't inflect them at all, and your listeners will merely look slightly puzzled. Give just the tiniest shade of emphasis, and you have a little gem.

+ + +

92—No matter what *faux pas* you may commit, it will pale into insignificance beside this one, as related by the lady herself:

"The moment this woman got on the train, I *knew* that I had met her somewhere before. I recalled vaguely that she was someone of social prominence, but I couldn't place her to save my life. Then catching my eye, she came rushing over, smiling effusively:

"'Well, my dear, how wonderful to find you here!' she exclaimed, following this with a stream of intimate reminiscenses. I clung to her every word, seeking some clew that would set me on the right track. Finally, in my half-dazed condition, I heard her say '. . . and my brother was mentioning you the other day!'

"That, at least, was something! So I took a long chance and said, 'Yes—yes—your brother! What—what is he doing now?'

"For a moment my companion looked at me in a dazed and startled condition. Then she stiffened. 'He is still,' she said icily, 'President of the United States!' "

+ + +

93—"My friends," said the jurist earnestly, "money is not all. It is not money that will mend a broken heart or reassemble the fragments of a dream. Money cannot brighten the hearth nor repair the portals of a shattered home." He paused, then continued softly, "I refer, of course, to Confederate money."

+ + +

94—The race is not always to the swift, nor the battle to the strong—but that's not a bad way to bet.

+ + +

95—"Jim," ordered the black boy's master, "I've found that this demijohn is empty, and the Colonel here and I are fairly perishing for a toddy. Throw a saddle on the fastest horse in the stable, light out for town and bring a supply of liquor back. If you hurry, you can make it in just forty minutes. Git goin' now!"

"Boss," said Jim solemnly, "I'se gone!"

"The roads are powerful muddy, Major," said the guest, "I'm afraid your boy can't make it on schedule."

"Don't you worry, Major," said the Colonel confidently, "that boy of mine is as punctual as they make 'em." He glanced at his watch, "Jim is just about galloping out of the stable right this minute."

Continuing with this theme, the Colonel proceeded mentally to follow the black boy on his important errand.

"He's passing through the swamp," suggested the Major, after an interval of five minutes.

"Yes," agreed the Colonel, "and now he's going past Donovan's blacksmith shop."

"He just raced across the bridge over Sugar Creek."

"The Methodist burial ground is right ahead of him."

"Fifteen minutes . . . ought to be gettin' into town by now."

"Now he's hitched, and runnin' into Jake Dudley's saloon."

"Eighteen minutes . . . Jake's probably fillin' up the jug by now."

"Yeah; an' drivin' the cork in."

"Now, I see Jim a-runnin' for his horse. Now, he's up and on the way home!"

"Twenty-one minutes and a half. . . . Watch that boy ridin' up Main Street!"

"He's passin' the outskirts!"

"Leavin' the buryin' ground behind!"

Drooling at the mouth, the two old men continued the mental race until—

"Thirty-nine minutes!" shouted the Major, "He must be galloping up the lane from the big road. Colonel, in just one minute from now, that boy will be standin' in the doorway—or I miss my guess."

And, sure enough, there stood Jim, panting from the effects of obvious exertion.

"Majah," said Jim, "fer de las' half hour er mo' I been lookin' fer de saddle fer dat hoss. . . . Seem lak I cain't fin' it nowheres."

+   +   +

96—When you have a long-drawn-out task before you, and some of the boys are beginning to lag a bit, this story may serve as a potent reminder:

A colored private from the South was getting pretty doggoned fed up with France and the rigors of war. He entertained a pronounced longing for possum, sweet potatoes and the pleasant indolence of his native state. Armistice had come and gone, yet supplies continued to arrive on the Brest docks, and there seemed an increasing and endless amount of work to be done. Finally, this boy ventured to broach his thoughts to the hard-boiled Negro sergeant:

"I'se gittin' plumb wore out," he complained, "wid all dis liftin' an' on-liftin'. Arm'stis' done come an' gone, an' dat's de same as de war bein' ovah. How comes dey don't ship me back what I come from? I only 'listed fo' de duration."

"Look heah boy," commanded the black boss, "De war is done ovah, like you say, but for sich ez you, de duration ain' hardly commenced yit."

+ + +

97—Here's a wow of a story to inspire a group toward some large undertaking:

A Chinese lad was peddling post cards at ten cents each.

"And what are you going to do with the money?" a kindly gentleman asked.

"I am raising a million dollars for the famine relief," the boy answered gravely.

The gentleman laughed. "A million dollars?" he cried. "Do you expect to raise it all by yourself?"

"No, sir," said the child earnestly, "there's another little boy helping me!"

+ + +

98—Demonstrating that worthwhile things are not accomplished without time and effort:

When James A. Garfield was president of Hiram College, in Ohio, he was approached by the father of a prospective pupil.

"Can't you simplify the course?" he asked. "My boy will never take all that in. He wants to get through by a shorter route."

"Certainly," answered Garfield, "I can arrange for that. It all depends, of course, on what you want to make of him. When God wants to make an oak, He takes a hundred years; but when He wants to make a squash, He requires only two months."

+   +   +

99—Irvin Cobb sets the stage for this one at the portals of Paradise. Approaching from left center are the shades of two mortals, seeking admission to Heavenly regions. One is a Southern colored boy, the other a Hebrew from New York's East Side.

Each gives satisfactory terrestial references, and both, it develops are entitled to dwell permanently among the Elect. Not only that, but there's a special blessing in store; what the theatrical folk might term "an extra added attraction." Each may have his dearest wish gratified.

"Please, sah, Mistah St. Peter," said the colored boy after a thoughtful interlude, "if it ain't puttin' you-all out too much, I craves me a million dollahs!"

No sooner said than the money-bags materialize before the somewhat dazed youth. Blinking, he stoops to pick them up.

"And you?" queried St. Peter, turning to the Hebrew.

"Vell," said the worldly-wise East-Sider, "I'm esking for twenty dollars worth o' phoney jewelry, and a half-hour alone with that nigger."

+ + +

100—While a Scotch minister was conducting religious services in an asylum for the insane, an inmate suddenly broke into the discourse:

"I say," he asked wildly, "have we got to listen to this?"

Confused and uncertain as to his future course, the minister turned to an attendant asking if he should proceed.

"Pay no heed to it," counselled the keeper. "That man has only one lucid moment every seven years."

+ + +

101—Here is a subtle, but very effective rebuke to the critics:

It was a hotly-contested baseball game between the teams of two county seat towns not exactly noted for their friendliness and neighborly affection. Anticipating a lively scrimmage, a traveling salesman decided to attend. He was surprised to observe no umpire in the usual position. Finally, he located an individual up in the grandstand, calling the balls and strikes. This procedure was so unusual that he ventured a query:

"Well, you see," explained the officiating gentleman, "the spectators used to beef so about my decisions, I thought if folks up in the grandstand could see every play so durned good, maybe I'd better come up here to do my umpirin'."

+ + +

102—A young lad was leafing through a current magazine and after looking for some time at a certain advertisement he finally asked his mother: "What does 'budget' mean? Is it something like a camel?"

She thought she had understood him correctly at first, but asked him to spell the word.

"B-u-d-g-e-t," he said, carefully spelling it out. "It says here—'See Egypt on a budget.'"

+ + +

103—The city fathers of Franklin, Massachusetts, wrote to Benjamin Franklin: "We have named our town after you, and we should like a donation of a sum of money from you in order that we may put a bell in the church steeple."

Replied Franklin: "I am very much honored, very glad indeed to send you a sum of money, only don't buy a bell with it. Buy a public library, because I have always preferred sense to sound." They bought books.

104—Walter Winchell tells of asking a friend how he fared at the races. The response: "I bet on a horse that if Paul Revere rode him—we'd all be talking with a British accent today."

+ + +

105—The minister's little daughter was never forgetful of her formal prayers and had been allowed the privilege of adding any original remarks that she saw fit. One night in the very late fall, at the close of her prayer she added, "And, dear Lord, please send the beautiful snow to keep the little flowers warm through the winter." Climbing into bed, she confided, "That's the time I fooled Him. I want the snow so I can go sliding with my new sled."

+ + +

106—It used to be that if a man possessed enough brass he could command an audience. In this modern day, before we give an ear, we demand that he convert the brass into tacks—and sharp-pointed ones, at that.

+ + +

107—The editor of a newspaper asked his readers to send in remarks on the subject, "Books that have helped me." One of the replies was: "My mother's cook book and my father's check book."

108—Orville Wright was reproached for not taking up the challenge of the Smithsonian Institute that it was Langley, not the Wrights, who was the first to fly.

"The trouble with you, Orville," said a friend, "is that you are too taciturn—you don't assert yourself enough. You should press-agentize more."

"My dear friend," Orville Wright answered, "the best talker and the worst flier among the birds is the parrot."

+ + +

109—The wife of an American official in Manchuria realized she and her husband were being shadowed. Returning unexpectedly to her hotel room one day, she surprised a man she knew to be one of several spies ransacking her trunks. With diplomatic thoughtfulness she saved his "face." Pretending she thought he was the room boy, she had him thoroughly dust, wash and clean the place, put away the clothes, count the laundry, pack and repack, until at the end of the day the man was completely exhausted. He was given a new assignment.

+ + +

110—A lordly Rolls Royce was followed through the congested traffic of New York by an antiquated Ford. The Rolls Royce stopped suddenly and the Ford crashed into it. A policeman rushed over and asked the driver of the Ford for his name and address.

"Paddy Murphy," was the reply.

"Begorra, is it now?" said the officer. "Hold on a minute while I give the other fellow a ticket for backin' into ye."

+ + +

111—Dale Carnegie was delivering an illustrated lecture on the Far East, a region he had never visited. He had learned the patter by rote, but the scenes were unfamiliar to him. Presently there came a view which, to save his neck, he could not identify. "Ah," said the suave lecturer, "here is another beautiful picture of the East. Let us enjoy it in silence."

+ + +

112—A classic story, told wherever military bandsmen congregate, concerns band units that are under the command of non-bandsmen officers.

It seems that a new lieutenant came on duty at an Army post. Bent on making a good impression, he inspected and inspected. At length he got around to the band, busy at a practice drill, at a moment when, in conformity with the notes on the music sheets, the trombone slides were moving at varying lengths.

"Stop!" shouted the lieutenant, "Close up those trombone slides! They look terrible—all out of line!"

113—Picasso, the world-renowned Spanish painter, was in France during the German occupation. His work was even appreciated by some of the Nazis there. One of the most prominent ones, Ambassador Otto Abetz, came to Picasso's studio one day and admired a recent painting showing the ruins of the bombed city of Guernica.

"This is wonderful," Abetz complimented. "Did you really do this?"

"No," Picasso told the Nazi representative. "You did."

+ + +

114—The hotel manager was interviewing a group of colored men who had come to apply for a job as porter.

"What," he asked of Goldenfleece Jones, "is the difference between courtesy and tact?"

Goldenfleece answered at once. "The las' place that I works I accidentally walk into a bathroom one day and theah a lady is sittin' in the bathtub. So I backs out and says, 'Beg-pahdon, suh.' Now that 'Beg-pahdon' was courtesy—but, man, that 'suh' was tact!"

+ + +

115—A basketball coach was addressing his team preparatory to an important contest.

"Now, boys," he concluded, "remember that basketball develops individuality, initiative and leadership. Now get out on the floor and do exactly as I told you."

116—Every public person is called upon at times to speak when he has nothing of particular interest to contribute. For such cases it is well to have a few stock anecdotes to provide a graceful out. Here is one you might add to your collection:

Sam Goldwyn, the motion picture mogul, had just scolded his bridge partner, Constance Bennett, the actress, for overbidding her hand.

"But how did I know you had nothing?" Miss Bennett asked.

"Why, Connie," said Sam reproachfully, "didn't you hear me keeping still?"

+ + +

117—Cordell Hull's caution, almost legendary, is best illustrated by a story from his Tennessee days:

A fellow townsman bet that he could make Judge Hull give him a direct answer to a question. He asked the time of day. Hull pulled out his own timepiece but replied: "What does your watch say?"

+ + +

118—He was telling her of his travels, and the things of international significance he had observed. At eleven, he was talking about the situation in Spain. At twelve, he started expounding on the influence of Russia. At one, he was in Great Britain. At two, her father started down-stairs, and daughter turned quickly to her suitor.

"And have you been in China, too?"

"Why, yes."

"Good; then I won't have to explain about the free-booters and the Open Door Policy."

+ + +

119—This story came from a lady who not so long ago was inducted into a tribe of Indians—a folk proverbially enamoured of tall talk.

On this solemn occasion, an old brave arose and said in stateliest Blackfoot: "I, Mountain Chief, am the last fighting warrior of my tribe and I fear nothing. I fear not the demons who rest in the snow on yonder peak, which once was ours. I fear not the devil spirits who lurk under the surface of this vast lake. I, Mountain Chief, who give thee this name, am the last fighting man of my tribe, and I fear nothing."

At this juncture a young and very modern brave snapped off this telltale translation: "This old boy, he say he ain't afraid of nothing."

+ + +

120—A young student of child behavior frequently delivered a lecture called "Ten Commandments for Parents." He married and became a father. The title of the lecture was altered to "Ten Hints for Parents." Another child arrived. The lecture became "Some Suggestions for Parents." A third child was born. The lecturer—so the story goes—stopped lecturing.

+ + +

121—One day the telephone rang in the home of Dr. Robert A. Millikan, the famous physicist, and Mrs. Millikan went to answer it. As she approached the telephone, she found that the colored maid had preceded her and was in the act of taking the call. Pausing to listen, she heard the maid say, "Yes, ma'am, this is where Dr. Millikan lives, but he ain't the kind of doctor that does anybody any good."

+ + +

122—"Anne," said the mistress of the house, "I notice you have been taking our empty grapefruit skins home with you. What do you do with them?"

The negro maid looked up at the mistress with a sheepish grin. "Yes, ma'am," she admitted, "I'se been carrying 'em home. I think they makes my garbage look so stylish."

+ + +

123—Recently a Canadian editor was in a gun plant where extremely fine tooling operations were being carried on.

"What are your tolerances on this job?" he asked a man at a lathe.

"One five-thousandth of an inch," replied the workman.

The figure conveyed little to the editor. He asked, "How fine is that?"

The workman, too, seemed puzzled. He called to his neighbor on the next machine. "Bill, how many five-thousandths are there in an inch?"

Bill scratched his head. "Gee, I don't know. But there must be millions of them."

+ + +

124—Charles Haddon Spurgeon was asked if the man who learned to play a cornet on Sunday would go to Heaven. The great preacher's reply was characteristic. Said he, "I don't see why he should not, but," after a pause, "I doubt whether the man next door will."

+ + +

125—A Wall Street broker whose firm occupies an entire floor in one of the big downtown hives became puzzled by the fact that the young lady elevator operator always said, "Watch your step!" when she stopped at his floor, even after a three-point landing. Finally he came right out and asked her why this was.

"I don't know, sir," she said. "All I know is that we have instructions to say 'Watch your step' at your floor."

126—As U. S. Ambassador, John G. Winant endeared himself to the British with his shy and unassuming manner. Called upon unexpectedly for a speech at a public function soon after he reached England, Mr. Winant rose, hesitated, finally murmured: "I knew I shouldn't have gotten up in the first place," and sat down. This address put the New Hampshire Yankee in solid with his British public.

+ + +

127—A long queue stood outside a theater in England where an opera company was playing for the season. Noticing the line, a woman passer-by approached and inquired.

"What are you people waiting for?"

"Tales of Hoffman," was the reply.

"Well," she remarked, joining the procession, "that'll do for me. I don't know how to cook 'em but my husband will eat anything."

+ + +

128—Goodwill, that old dependable quality that business strives for, has been defined by a somewhat cynical lawyer as follows:

"Goodwill is an unnamed malady with which the public is inflicted, composed, among other things, of habit, inertia, and fear of contact with strangers, which causes the victim to sit at the same greasy-spoon lunch counter day after day rather than go next door and enjoy superior fare and comfort at less cost."

+ + +

129—A young playwright once brought his masterpiece to George Bernard Shaw for an opinion. After listening to the first act, Shaw fell asleep. The young author was indignant.

"Mr. Shaw! Mr. Shaw!" he said sharply.

G. B. S. stirred. "Uh, yes? What is it?" he asked.

"May I remind you that I came here to get your comment?"

"My dear boy," yawned Shaw, "sleep is a comment."

+ + +

130—A schoolkid's terse comment on a scheduled classroom talk: "Even if it's lousy, it will be better than arithmetic."

+ + +

131—A simple lesson in humility was illustrated not long ago in a cartoon appearing in a leading metropolitan newspaper. It pictured a young woman in graduation cap and gown, with the inevitable diploma and an expression of self-satisfied dignity and assurance. Before her stood the

World with an expression of age-old wisdom and experience. "Well, who have we here?" the World asked.

"You evidently don't know me," the young lady replied, "I am Virginia Cordelia Smith, A. B."

"Ah," said the World, "come with me and I will teach you the rest of your alphabet."

+ + +

132—From the dark came the voice of the sentry, "Halt! Who goes there?"

"An American," was the reply.

"Is that so? Well, advance and recite the second verse of 'The Star Spangled Banner.' "

"I don't know it."

"Proceed, American."

+ + +

133—A certain English novelist came over to the United States to do a lecture circuit. Addressing a midwestern audience, he began to realize, after about fifteen minutes, that he wasn't being listened to very attentively. He interrupted his dull talk and announced that he was going out for a ten minute smoke.

"Please gather your wits while I am out," he urged them in his best professional manner.

When he returned he found a neatly penned note on the rostrum: "We gathered our wits."

134—It was during negotiations between the United States and China at the close of the "Boxer Rebellion." Following a conference between Secretary of State John Hay, and the Minister of China, Mr. Wu, reporters asked an attache of the State Department to explain the purpose of the negotiations. The attache replied:

"Well, I'm not quite sure, as Mr. Hay was a bit hazy, and Mr. Wu a trifle woozy."

+ + +

135—There were three people in the British railway compartment—an old lady and two men. Suddenly one of the men said, "25," and the other immediately burst into laughter. When he had ceased chuckling he called out, "121," and the other man then roared with laughter. This went on for some time. No sooner would one call a number than the other would laugh.

The old lady, doubting the sanity of her two companions, turned to them and said, "Excuse me, but I don't see anything funny in shouting a number."

"It's all right, madam," one replied. "We are commercial travelers, and we know all our jokes by number."

+ + +

136—A soprano, aspiring to grand opera, asked a German music professor to hear her. He played the accompaniment and listened to her for a few minutes, but she sang so far off key that he finally slammed down the piano cover and refused to continue.

"What's the matter?" asked the young woman. "Don't you like my singing?"

"Der trouble mit your singing, madam," asserted the professor, "is dot veder I play on der vite keys or der black ones, you sing in der cracks."

+   +   +

137—A state official, accompanied by a friend, arrived at his office one morning and found a number of men waiting for him in the anteroom. He paused as he passed through, and related an ancient, rather pointless joke.

Inside his private office, the friend remarked, "Say that was a terrible old chestnut you pulled out there."

"I know it," was the complacent reply, "but I had to find out how many of those fellows were here just to ask favors."

"And did you?" inquired the friend.

"Oh, yes," said the official, "they were the ones who laughed."

+   +   +

138—A well-known novelist sold the cinema rights of one of his novels to a certain motion picture producer, and when the picture adaptation was completed, the producer submitted it to the novelist for his okay.

With growing amazement, the writer perused the scenario of his book, and at one point exclaimed, "What on earth is this?"

Looking over the novelist's shoulder at the scene indicated, the producer studied the lines. "Oh, yes," he explained. "In your novel there was a girl in that scene, but in the picture we made her a boat."

+   +   +

139—The speaker was much annoyed by a man in his audience who coughed and sneezed and blew his nose almost constantly. Finally, the speaker could stand it no longer. As politely as he could he suggested to the brother who was having so much discomfort that a visit to the open air might be good for his cold.

"I haven't any cold," came the answer. "I'm just allergic to applesauce."

+   +   +

140—She insisted on taking innumerable frocks with her and they arrived at the station loaded with luggage.

"I wish," said the husband thoughtfully, "that we'd brought the piano."

"You needn't try to be sarcastic," came the frigid reply. "It's not a bit funny."

"I'm not trying to be funny," he explained, sadly, "I left the tickets on it."

141—William Lyon Phelps once said that the highest compliment he ever received was paid him by one of Dr. James R. Angell's children. While he was preaching in the Yale Chapel, this little girl sat with her father and mother in the presidential pew. When he had finished, she said: "Mama, during Professor Phelps' sermon 1 didn't itch once."

+ + +

142—Dr. Burris Jenkins, pastor of a Kansas City church was a last-minute substitute speaker at a neighborhood gathering. The chairman explained that the committee had had a great disappointment. They had failed in their efforts to secure an Admiral. The Governor, too, had been unable to attend. And so on down the list, but here, he concluded, was Dr. Jenkins as a gap-plugger.

Dr. Jenkins, who had never had just that sort of an introduction, said he felt like a bundle of old clothing stuffed in a crevice to replace a broken window pane.

After the meeting, the first to reach the speaker was a dear old lady.

"Oh, Dr. Jenkins," she said, "you're not old rags; you're a pane!"

+ + +

143—A witty writer, speaking of a dull and uninteresting book given to him by a fellow craftsman, remarked, "It took Sir William Ramsay sixteen years to discover helium; the Curies thirty years to find radium; yet in five minutes, you produce tedium."

+   +   +

144—A definition which quite often fits the occasion: A co-ordinator is a man who brings organized chaos out of regimented confusion.

+   +   +

145—A minister was asked if he was making many new friends in his new charge.

"Well," he replied, smiling, "I must say I noticed quite a few nodding acquaintances in my congregation this morning."

+   +   +

146—A sailor had broken with his girl. After ignoring several letters requesting the return of her photograph, one came threatening to complain to the captain. Deciding to squelch her for all time, he borrowed all the pictures of girls available on the ship, sending them to her in a large bundle with the note: "Pick yours out; I've forgotten what you look like."

+   +   +

147—A New York drama critic, famous for his acid wit and indigestion, had unwisely packed away a heavy dinner before the opening of a certain show. To make matters worse, the show proved very bad. Finally a loud burp escaped the critic's lips. A young lady, seated near by, suggested politely: "Would you mind waiting until you leave the theatre to give your review?"

+ + +

148—A certain happily married college professor, delivering a graduation address, gave this sage counsel:

"Gentlemen, many of you will marry. Let me entreat you to be kind to your wives. Be patient with them. When you are going out together, do not worry if your wife is not ready at the appointed time. Have a good book near by. Read it while you wait. And, gentlemen, I assure you that you will be astonished at the amount of information you will acquire."

+ + +

149—Formula for success: Stand up to be seen; speak up to be heard; shut up to be appreciated.

+ + +

150—A Hungarian aristocrat, while devouring a quick lunch between trains, was recognized by a boorish acquaintance.

"My dear Count! How are you?"

"Umph."

"And how is the Countess?"

"Dead."

"How shocking! It must be terrible for your daughter."

"She's dead."

"But your son—"

"Dead! Everybody's dead when I'm eating!"

+　+　+

151—A New York restaurant man secured the biggest fish bowl he could find, filled it with water and put it in his window with this sign: "Filled with invisible goldfish from the Argentine." It took seventeen policemen to hold back the people.

+　+　+

152—Here is one of those crazy things that make the rounds periodically.

Sir Lancelot was lost one dark night in a deep woods. He wandered about helplessly and after some hours encountered a handsome St. Bernard dog. The dog attached himself to Sir Lancelot, and they went on together for some time. Then the knight, exhausted, sat on the back of the animal. It dutifully took him straightway to a tavern. Sir Lancelot knocked at the door. "Could you give me bed and board?" he inquired of the proprietor.

The tavern keeper peered out into the darkness. "Who am I to turn out a knight on a dog like this?" he answered.

153—One afternoon, while three hermits were sitting in their community cave, a beautiful girl and her setter went past the entrance.

A year later, the first hermit remarked, "Some girl!"

Another year went by. Then the second hermit said, "And some dog!"

Whereupon the third hermit got up disgustedly. "I'm getting out of here," he said. "All this chatter is driving me crazy."

+ + +

154—J. B. Coleman, a French minister of finance in the 17th century, laid down this rule for taxation: "The art of taxation consists of so plucking the goose as to obtain the largest amount of feathers with the least possible amount of hissing."

+ + +

155—Refinement: The ability to yawn without opening the mouth.

+ + +

156—"Yes, I am a self-made man," boasted the magnate.

The quiet gentleman in the clerical collar looked at him reflectively.

"Sir," he replied, "you relieve the Lord of a great responsibility."

157—Into the office of an area rent control adminis-
trator walked a worried man. "Who's my landlord?" he
asked a clerk.

"He's the man you pay your rent to," he was told.

"I don't pay no rent." The man explained that nine
years ago he had moved into a vacant house.

"Well, then if that's the case, what is your complaint?"

"My roof leaks," replied the man, "and if it isn't fixed
pretty soon, I'm goin' to move out."

+   +   +

158—A minister was ill and asked his wife to take his
temperature. By mistake she put a barometer into his
mouth. When she took it out, he asked, "How does it
read?"

She answered, "Dry and windy!"

+   +   +

159—A teacher found herself explaining fractions to
one of the little girls who always seemed to look a little
bit drugged when the subject came up in class. The teacher
tried to explain the whole business clearly in various ingenious ways, using progressive school symbols, but there
was little response. "Don't you understand at all, Ethel?"
she asked wearily after she had exhausted her supply of
tricks.

"Oh, I understand all right," said Ethel airily. "I just
don't happen to agree with you."

160—The exuberant young author, displaying a confidence rather foreign to the craft, approached a busy editor. "How many words," he asked, "are there in a novel?"

"Why," responded the editor, "about sixty thousand."

"Oh," said the author with a sigh of relief, "then my book is finished."

+ + +

161—A Maine hunter captured an elk, and being an enterprising chap, conceived the idea of putting it on exhibition to make some money.

Among the prospects at the box office one afternoon, the exhibitor noted a man, his wife, and so many children that he grew dizzy trying to tally them.

"Are they all yours?" he asked incredulously.

"Oh, yes," beamed the citizen. "Sixteen of 'em. Do I get a special family rate?"

"Well, I'll tell you," pondered the owner of the exhibit. "I'm going to let the whole bunch of you in free. I figure it's worth as much for my elk to see your family as it is for your family to see my elk."

+ + +

162—Teacher was taking her class to the zoo for a little first-hand observation. Pointing to a deer, she asked little Johnny to identify it.

When he showed some signs of indecision, the teacher prompted helpfully: "Now, now, Johnny, I'm sure you know. What does your mother call your father?"

"Aw," said tough little Johnny, "don't tell me that's a louse!"

+ + +

163—"I had the nicest dream last night," announced little Barbara at breakfast. Duly urged, she continued: "I dreamed that everything I said was important."

+ + +

164—A city boy, visiting his country cousin was walking through the pasture when he heard a peculiar buzzing sound. He looked around to find out what it was. "Come away from there!" the cousin shouted. "It's a rattlesnake! If you go near it, it will strike."

"Gosh," said the city boy, "do they have unions too?"

+ + +

165—One of the questions asked in an examination on stock-raising was, "Name four different kinds of sheep."

An inspired youth answered: "Black sheep, white sheep, Mary's little lamb and the hydraulic ram."

+ + +

166—A woman, critically injured in a traffic accident had been rushed to a hospital.

"Did you hold a mirror to her face to see if she was still breathing?" an attending doctor asked.

"Oh, yes," said the young interne. "She opened one eye, gasped, and reached for her powder puff."

+ + +

167—Gossip is the art of saying nothing in a way that leaves nothing unsaid.

+ + +

168—Dario, owner of the night club La Martinique tells of visiting a Danube cafe where gypsy musicians played. The gypsy "collector" passed among the listeners soliciting contributions with his outstretched right palm. He held his left fist clenched tightly.

"Why the fist?" Dario asked.

"So I do not steal money," the collector explained. "My chief, he put a fly in my left hand. When I go back to him the fly must still be there, alive—as proof that I have not opened my left hand—as proof that I did not steal."

+ + +

169—A northern passenger on a small Mississippi river steamboat in the deep south was considerably perturbed when he heard the captain say his craft would be delayed some four or five hours, pending arrival of some expected cargo. He sought out the officer and expressed his regret that the craft would be late in arriving at New Orleans.

"Late?" said the captain. "Why I reckon we'll get in about on time."

"But I just heard you say we'd be delayed here for four or five hours."

"Shucks," said the placid riverman, "we don't run on a schedule as close as all that."

+   +   +

170—"There are two things necessary for success, my boy," cautioned a fond father. "They are honesty and sagacity."

"What is honesty, father?"

"No matter what happens, or how adversely it affects you, always keep your word, once you have given it."

"And sagacity?"

"Never give it."

+   +   +

171—On entering a movie theater, the patron was taken in tow by an usher who led him skyward on ramp after ramp to the floor level of the top balcony, where he stopped and pointed upward into the grayness.

"You'll find a seat up there somewhere. This is as far up as I go. Above this level, my nose bleeds."

172—A colonel was speaking at a dinner given in his honor before embarking for Africa.

"I thank you," he concluded, "for your kind wishes regarding my welfare, and I want you to know that when I am far away, surrounded by ugly, grinning savages, I shall always think of you."

+ + +

173—A little lad paused at the window for a last look at the starry heaven before he said his good-night prayers.

"Mummy, will I go to heaven some time?"

"Yes, dear, if you love Jesus."

"And will you be there?" he asked again.

"I hope so, and Daddy'll be there too."

The little fellow shook his head emphatically. "My Daddy won't be there; he couldn't leave the store."

+ + +

174—A panhandler, holding out two hats, explained: "Business is so good I opened a branch office!"

+ + +

175—Walking up the street, a Federal officer heard frightful screams coming from a house. He ran to investigate; found a small boy had swallowed a quarter. His mother, not knowing what to do, was frantic.

The man caught the little fellow by the heels and holding him up, gave him a few shakes. The coin dropped to the floor.

"Well," exclaimed the grateful mother, "you certainly know what to do. Are you a doctor?"

"No, madam," replied the official, "I'm a collector of internal revenue."

+ + +

176—Two members were examining a newly-refurbished motto, in the lobby of their club. It read:

"The faults of our brothers we write upon the sand; their virtues upon tablets of love and memory."

At this moment there was a loud noise in the street outside.

"What was that?" inquired one.

"Probably," said his cynical companion, "a truck bringing up another load of sand."

+ + +

177—Everyone can give pleasure in some way. One person may do it by coming into a room, and another by going out.

+ + +

178—On a state visit to Bismarck, Benjamin Disraeli, the great statesman, observed that the Iron Chancellor always managed to get rid of unwelcome visitors quickly. He asked Bismarck the secret.

"Nothing is more simple," said Bismarck. "When my wife thinks people have wasted enough of my time, she tells my valet to come and inform me that the Emperor wishes to see me immediately. That always works admirably."

There was a knock at the door, the valet entered and spoke: "His Majesty wishes to speak to Your Highness."

+ + +

179—The itching sensation that some people mistake for ambition is merely inflammation of the wishbone.

+ + +

180—The Quaker had heard a strange noise in the night, and waking, found a burglar ransacking the kitchen. He took his fowling piece and called from the landing of the kitchen stairs, in plain sight of the intruder: "Friend, I would do thee no harm for the world and all that is in it—but thee standest in the spot where I am about to shoot." The burglar fled.

+ + +

181—A veteran church deacon announced to an associate the other day that he had developed a device that was bound to make him rich. "Every church," he said confidently, "is sure to want this patented collection-plate of mine."

"What's the special feature?"

"Well, you see, it works like this: Coins fall through slots of different sizes. Dollars, half-dollars and quarters fall on velvet; dimes, nickels and pennies drop on a Chinese bell!"

+ + +

182—An ordinary man will simply say, "Two and two make four"—and let it go at that. But not your orator. He will clear his throat, lift up his hands and say—

"My countrymen, when in the course of human events, it becomes necessary to take a number of the 2nd denomination and add to it the little figure 2, I make bold to assert—and I do assert without fear of successful contradiction—that as long as there is a good and just God in Heaven, visiting His many blessings on the beautiful women, the stalwart men and lovely little children now assembled before me, the result will invariably be 4!"

+ + +

183—The pompous president of a midwestern bank was making a speech to his directors—one of his usual show-off talks. He used a French phrase, and stumbled a bit as he noted the cold eye of a statistical expert.

He paused, beamed just a little and said, "That's the way the word is pronounced, isn't it?"

The expert leaned back in his chair and replied: "Yes—frequently."

184—The late William Allen White attended a testimonial dinner, during which the toastmaster, in introducing speakers, spoke longer than the persons introduced. When finally it came White's turn he began: "There are times when I enjoy playing with huge numbers. Right now, statistics regarding toastmasters keep running through my mind. It just struck me that if every toastmaster were placed end to end—it would be a really excellent thing."

+ + +

185—A colored church congregation had met to pray for rain to release a long dry spell. The preacher looked severely at his flock and said:

"Brothers and Sisters, yo' all know why we is here. Now what I wants to know is—where is yo' umbrellas?"

+ + +

186—A man was giving some advice to his son. At the end of a rather stern lecture, he said: "Now, my boy, you understand perfectly what I mean?"

"Yes," replied the boy, "what it boils down to is this: If I do well it's because of heredity, and if I fail it's my own fault."

+ + +

187—Robert St. John, the author, was standing in the lobby of the NBC studios, in Chicago's Merchandise Mart, where his luxuriant beard attracted considerable attention.

A woman visitor asked a page the identity of the owner of that hirsute splendor.

"That's St. John," she was told.

"Um-m," mused the visitor, turning again to the beard. "Here for the Baptist Convention, I presume."

+ + +

188—"The process of thinking draws the blood from the feet to the head," an educator informs us. This explains, perhaps, why, in so many cases, if you think twice about a proposition you get cold feet."

+ + +

189—With tears in her eyes his wife exclaimed: "I know you don't love me—you've forgotten my birthday!"

"Darling," replied the quick thinker, "I am more sorry than I can say, but it is really your fault."

"My fault?" she exclaimed. "How can that be?"

He took her hand in his. "How can I remember your birthday," he asked, "when there is never anything about you to remind me that you are a day older than you were a year ago?"

+ + +

190—An officer of the law chanced upon a man pacing the sidewalk at 3 a. m. Being alert to the responsibilities of his post, he paused to inquire into the unusual situation.

"Oh, it's all right, officer," he was assured. "I live here. I forgot my keys and I'm waiting for my children to come home and let me in."

+ + +

191—In a civil service examination given in New York sometime ago, one of the questions asked was the following: "If a man buys an article for $12.25 and sells it for $9.75, does he gain or lose by the transaction?"

One of our modern young sweet things, with good looks unmarred by brains, after studying for a while, gave the following answer: "He gains on the cents but loses on the dollars."

+ + +

192—In the opinion of many speakers, the ideal situation involves speaking on an empty stomach—to a well-fed audience.

Caruso, who always abstained from food before an opera performance, would illustrate his point by striking an empty crystal goblet with a knife. A fine musical note, clear and strong, would result. Then, filling the glass, he would strike it again, producing a dull, flat, unlovely sound.

193—A minister of Scotch descent, rather noted for his close calculations also operated a small farm in Vermont.

One day he observed his hired man sitting idly by the plow, as the horses took a needed rest. This rather shocked the good man's sense of economy. After all, he was paying the man 25c an hour. So he said, gently, but reproachfully, "John, wouldn't it be a good plan for you to have a pair of shears and be trimming these bushes while the horses are resting?"

"That it would," replied John agreeably. "And might I suggest, your reverence, that you take a peck of potatoes into the pulpit and peel 'em during the anthem."

+   +   +

194—A good illustration of theory versus practice is the story of a young couple who had a new baby and had armed themselves with a formidable tome on child care. One night the infant was wailing and the parents stood by its crib, peering through the index of their book and eyeing their little one with trepidation. Came a voice from the nursery door where their Irish cook stood in her nightgown: "If I was youse," she said, "I'd put down the book and pick up the baby."

+   +   +

195—There are two sides to everything—including a sheet of flypaper. But it makes a lot of difference to the fly which side he's on.

196—The bride tottered up the aisle on the arm of her father, who was wheeled in his armchair by three of his great-grandchildren. She was arrayed in white and carried a big bouquet of white rosebuds; her hair, though gray, was bobbed, and she smiled and nodded to acquaintances.

The groom was able to walk, aided by two handsome mahogany crutches. His head was bald, and his false teeth chattered a little nervously.

And so they were married—the couple who waited until they could afford to get married.

+ + +

197—In that trying period preceding the program, the visiting lecturer was being entertained by a local social leader of the fluttery type. Hard-pressed for conversational topics, she at length inquired, "And do you believe in clubs for women?"

"Oh, yes," said the lecturer. "Yes, indeed," and then pausing significantly, "but of course only when kindness fails."

+ + +

198—A noted educator was addressing students in chapel at the beginning of a school year. He expressed his gratification in learning that the school had enrolled the largest freshman class in its history. And then turning to the lesson for the day, he read these words from the third Psalm: "Lord, how they are increased that trouble me!"

+ + +

199—Mike, the foreman of a logging camp employing a hundred men and a couple of women cooks, was inclined to be extremely verbose in his reports to the management. Finally, after several broad hints, an executive issued positive orders.

"Mike," he said, "I haven't time to read page after page of minute details. Boil it down. Give me the picture in percentages; that's all that really matters."

So, in his next report, Mike wrote: "Last month, 1% of the men married 50% of the women."

+ + +

200—Three small boys were bragging about the prowess of their respective dads.

"My dad," said one, "writes a few short lines on a piece of paper, calls it a poem—and gets $10 for it."

"My dad," said another, "makes some dots on a piece of paper, calls it a song—and they pay him $25 for it."

"That's nothing," said the third. "My father writes a sermon on a sheet of paper, gets up in the pulpit and reads it and it takes four men to bring in the money!"

Popular Poems for Public Speakers

THE LADIES

I've taken my fun where I've found it;
I've rouged an' I've ranged in my time;
I've 'ad my pickin' o' sweethearts,
An' four o' the lot was prime.
One was an 'art-caste widow,
One was a woman at Prome,
One was the wife of a jemadar-sais, (head-groom)
An' one is a girl at 'ome.

Now I aren't no 'and with the ladies,
For, takin' 'em all along,
You never can say till you've tried 'em,
An' then you are like to be wrong.
There's times when you'll think that you mightn't,
There's times when you'll know that you might;
But the things you will learn from the Yellow an' Brown,
They'll 'elp you a lot with the White!

I was a young un at 'Oogli,
Shy as a girl to begin;
Aggie de Castrer she made me,
An' Aggie was clever as sin;

Older than me, but my first un—
More like a mother she were—
Showed me the way to promotion an' pay,
An' I learned about women from 'er!

Then I was ordered to Burma,
Actin' in charge o' Bazar,
An' I got me a tiddy live 'eathen
Through buyin' supplies off 'er pa.
Funny an' yellow an' faithful—
Doll in a teacup she were—
But we lived on the square, like a true-married pair,
An' I learned about women from 'er!

Then we was shifted to Neemuch
(Or I might ha' been keepin' 'er now),
An' I took with a shiny she-devil,
The wife a nigger at Mhow;
'Taught me the gipsy-folks' *bolee;* (slang)
Kind o' volcano she were,
For she knifed me one night 'cause I wished she was white,
And I learned about women from 'er!

Then I come 'ome in a trooper,
'Long of a kid o' sixteen—
'Girl from a convent at Meerut,
The straightest I ever 'ave seen.

Love at first sight was 'er trouble,
She didn't know what it were;
An' I wouldn't do such, 'cause I like 'er too much,
But—I learned about women from 'er!

I've taken my fun where I've found it,
An' now I must pay for my fun,
For the more you 'ave know o' the others
The less will you settle to one;
An' the end of it's sittin' and thinking',
An' dreamin' Hell-fires to see;
So be warned by my lot (which I know you will not),
An' learn about women from me!

—Rudyard Kipling.

THE FACE ON THE BARROOM FLOOR

This classic, by Hugh D'Arcy, was first printed in 1887, and titled *The Face Upon the Floor*. It is amusing to note that it was never intended to point out the perils of strong drink, but merely to portray the degradation of an artist tortured by the loss of his sweetheart. The poem was seized by the W.C.T.U., and later the Anti-Saloon League, the title altered, and millions of copies distributed as propaganda.

"If I thought my poem had done anything to help Pro-
hibition," said D'Arcy, in 1925, "I would go take a running
jump into the Hudson."

The poem follows the familiar "my-pal-stole-my-gal"
theme. The artist, "gone gutter," drifts into a barroom,
begging a drink. Fortified by a swig of whiskey, he tells
his tale in too-many verses.

'Twas a balmy summer evening, and a goodly crowd was
    there,
Which well-nigh filled Joe's barroom, on the corner of the
    square;
And as songs and witty stories came through the open
    door,
A vagabond crept slowly in and posed upon the floor.

"Where did it come from?" someone said. "The wind has
    blown it in."
"What does it want?" another cried. "Some whiskey, rum
    or gin?"
"Here, Toby, sic 'em, if your stomach's equal to the work—
I wouldn't touch him with a fork, he's filthy as a Turk."

This badinage the poor wretch took with stoical good
    grace;
In fact, he smiled as tho' he thought he'd struck the proper
    place.

"Come, boys, I know there's kindly hearts among so good
    a crowd—.
To be in such good company would make a deacon proud.

"Give me a drink—that's what I want—I'm out of funds,
    you know,
When I had cash to treat the gang this hand was never
    slow.
What? You laugh as if you thought this pocket never held
    a sou;
I once was fixed as well, my boys, as any one of you.

"There, thanks, that's braced me nicely; God bless you one
    and all;
Next time I pass this good saloon I'll make another call.
Give you a song? No, I can't do that; my singing days are
    past;
My voice is cracked, my throat's worn out, and my lungs
    are going fast.

"I'll tell you a funny story, and a fact, I promise, too..
Say! Give me another whiskey, and I'll tell you what I'll
    do—
That I was ever a decent man not one of you would think;
But I was, some four or five years back. Say, give me an-
    other drink.

"Fill her up, Joe, I want to put some life into my frame—
Such little drinks to a bum like me are miserably tame;
Five fingers—there, that's the scheme—and corking whis-
    key, too.
Well, here's luck, boys, and landlord, my best regards to
    you.

"You've treated me pretty kindly and I'd like to tell you
    how
I came to be the dirty sot you see before you now.
As I told you, once I was a man, with muscle, frame, and
    health,
And but for a blunder ought to have made considerable
    wealth.

"I was a painter—not one that daubed on bricks and wood,
But an artist, and for my age, was rated pretty good.
I worked hard at my canvas, and was bidding fair to rise,
For gradually I saw the star of fame before my eyes.

"I made a picture perhaps you've seen, 'tis called the 'Chase
    of Fame.'
It brought me fifteen hundred pounds and added to my
    name,
And then I met a woman—now comes the funny part—
With eyes that petrified my brain, and sunk into my heart.

"Why don't you laugh? 'Tis funny that the vagabond you
  see

Could ever love a woman, and expect her love for me;
But 'twas so, and for a month or two, her smiles were freely
  given,
And when her loving lips touched mine, it carried me to
  Heaven.

"Boys, did you ever see a girl for whom your soul you'd
  give,
With a form like the Milo Venus, too beautiful to live;
With eyes that would beat the Koh-i-noor, and a wealth of
  chestnut hair?
If so, 'twas she, for there never was another half so fair.

"I was working on a portrait, one afternoon in May,
Of a fair-haired boy, a friend of mine, who lived across the
  way.
And Madeline admired it, and much to my surprise,
Said she'd like to know the man that had such dreamy eyes.

"It didn't take long to know him, and before the month
  had flown
My friend had stole my darling, and I was left alone;
And ere a year of misery had passed above my head,
The jewel I had treasured so had tarnished and was dead.

"That's why I took to drink, boys. Why, I never see you
   smile,
I thought you'd be amused, and laughing all the while.

Why, what's the matter, friend? There's a tear-drop in
   your eye,
Come, laugh like me. 'Tis only babes and women that
   should cry.

"Say, boys, if you give me just another whiskey I'll be glad,
And I'll draw right here a picture of the face that drove me
   mad.
Give me that piece of chalk with which you mark the base-
   ball score—
You shall see the lovely Madeline upon the barroom floor."

Another drink, and with chalk in hand, the vagabond
   began
To sketch a face that well might buy the soul of any man.
Then, as he placed another lock upon the shapely head,
With a fearful shriek, he leaped and fell across the pic-
   ture—dead.

                              —*H. Antoine D'Arcy.*

THE BALLAD OF YUKON JAKE

(The Hermit of Shark Tooth Shoal)

Oh the North Countree is a hard countree
   That mothers a bloody brood;
And its icy arms hold hidden charms
   For the greedy, the sinful and lewd.

And strong men rust, from the gold and lust
   That sears the Northland soul,
But the wickedest born, from the pole to the Horn,
   Is the Hermit of Shark Tooth Shoal.

Now Jacob Kaime was the Hermit's name,
   In the days of his pious youth,
Ere he cast a smirch on the Baptist church
   By betraying a girl named Ruth.

But now men quake at Yukon Jake,
   The Hermit of Shark Tooth Shoal,
For that is the name that Jacob Kaime
   Is known by from Nome to the Pole.

He was just a boy and the parson's joy
   (Ere he fell for the gold and the muck),
And he learned to pray, with the hogs and hay
   On a farm near Keokuk.

But a Service tale of illicit kale—
   And whiskey and women wild—
Drained the morals clean as a soup-tureen
   From this poor but honest child.

He longed for the bite of a Yukon night
   And the Northern Light's weird flicker,
For a game of stud in the frozen mud,
   And the taste of raw red licker.

He wanted to mush along in the slush
   With a team of huskie hounds,
And to fire his gat at a beaver hat
   And knock it out of bounds.

So he left his home for the hell-town Nome
   On Alaska's ice-ribbed shores,
And he learned to curse and to drink and worse—
   Till the rum dripped from his pores.

When the boys on a spree were drinking it free
   In a Malamute saloon
And Dan McGrew and his dangerous crew
   Shot craps with the piebald coon:

When the Kid on his stool banged away like a fool
   At a jag-time melody
And the bar-keep vowed to the hardboiled crowd
   That he'd cree-mate Sam McGee—

Then Jacob Kaime, who had taken the name
   Of Yukon Jake, the Killer,
Would rake the dive with his forty-five
   Till the atmosphere grew chiller.

With a sharp command he'd make 'em stand
   And deliver their hard-earned dust,
Then drink the bar dry of rum and rye,
   As a Klondike bully must.

Without coming to blows he would tweak the nose
   Of Dangerous Dan McGrew
And becoming bolder, throw over his shoulder
   The Lady that's known as Lou.

Oh, tough as steak was Yukon Jake—
   Hardboiled as a picnic egg.
He washed his shirt in the Klondike dirt,
   And drank his rum by the keg.

In fear of their lives (or because of their wives)
   He was shunned by the best of his pals;
An outcast he, from the comraderie
   Of all but wild animals.

So he bought him the whole of Shark Tooth Shoal,
   A reef in the Bering Sea,
And he lived by himself on a sea lion's shelf
   In lonely iniquity.

But miles away, in Keokuk, Ia.
  Did a ruined maiden fight
To remove the smirch from the Baptist Church
  By bringing the heathen Light.

And the Elders declared that all would be squared
  If she carried the holy words
From her Keokuk home to the hell-town Nome
  To save those sinful birds.

So, two weeks later, she took a freighter,
  For the gold-cursed land near the Pole,
But Heaven ain't made for a lass that betrayed—
  She was wrecked on Shark Tooth Shoal!

All hands were tossed in the sea and lost—
  All but the maiden Ruth,
Who swam to the edge of the sea lion's ledge
  Where abode the love of her youth.

He was hunting a seal for his evening meal
  (He handled a mean harpoon)
When he saw at his feet not something to eat,
  But a girl in a frozen swoon.

Whom he dragged to his lair by her dripping hair,
  And he rubbed her knees with gin.
To his surprise she opened her eyes
  And revealed—his Original Sin!

His eight months' beard grew stiff and weird
   And it felt like a chestnut burr,
And he swore by his gizzard—and the Arctic blizzard
   That he'd do right by her.

But the cold sweat froze on the end of her nose
   Till it gleamed like a Tecla pearl,
While her bright hair fell like a flame from hell
   Down the back of the grateful girl.

But a hopeless rake was Yukon Jake
   The Hermit of Shark Tooth Shoal!
And the dizzy maid he rebetrayed
   And wrecked her immortal soul!

Then he rowed her ashore with a broken oar,
   And he sold her to Dan McGrew
For a huskie dog and a hot egg-nog—
   As rascals are wont to do.

Now ruthless Ruth is a maid uncouth
   With scarlet cheeks and lips,
And she sings rough songs to the drunken throngs
   That come from the sealing ships.

For a rouge-stained kiss from this infamous miss
   They will give a seal's sleek fur,
Or perhaps a sable, if they are able;
   It's much the same to her....

Oh, the North Countree is a hard countree,
   That mothers a bloody brood;
And its icy arms hold hidden charms
   For the greedy, the sinful and lewd.

And strong men rust, from the gold and lust
   That sears the Northland soul,
But the wickedest born from the Pole to the Horn
   Is the Hermit of Shark Tooth Shoal!

—Edward E. Paramore, Jr.

CASEY AT THE BAT

As you well know, this is the poem that De Wolf Hopper
made famous, through innumerable recitals. Or would it,
perhaps, be more to the point to say that the poem made
Hopper famous? In any case, we have rather lost sight of
the fact that the ballad was foundationed in fact. There
was a Mighty Casey—indeed there yet is, for he is still
living in Washington, D. C. Mr. Casey, luminary of a
minor league at the turn of the century, declares that in
the poem Author Thayer has much maligned him. He
was, he is careful to explain, a pitcher—and was never supposed to hit:

It looked extremely rocky for the Mudville nine that day,
The score stood four to six with but an inning left to play.

And so, when Cooney died at first, and Burrows did the
 same,
A pallor wreathed the features of the patrons of the game.
A straggling few got up to go, leaving there the rest,
With that hope which springs eternal within the human
 breast.
For they thought if only Casey could get a whack at that,
They'd put up even money with Casey at the bat.
But Flynn preceded Casey, and likewise so did Blake,
And the former was a pudding and the latter was a fake;
So on that stricken multitude a death-like silence sat,
For there seemed but little chance of Casey's getting to the
 bat.
But Flynn let drive a single to the wonderment of all,
And the much despised Blakey tore the cover off the ball,
And when the dust had lifted and they saw what had oc-
 curred,
There was Blakey safe on second, and Flynn a-hugging
 third.
Then from the gladdened multitude went up a joyous yell,
It bounded from the mountain top and rattled in the dell,
It struck upon the hillside, and rebounded on the flat,
For Casey, mighty Casey, was advancing to the bat.
There was ease in Casey's manner as he stepped into his
 place,
There was pride in Casey's bearing and a smile on Casey's
 face,

And when responding to the cheers he lightly doffed his
hat,

No stranger in the crowd could doubt, 'twas Casey at the
bat.

Ten thousand eyes were on him as he rubbed his hands
with dirt,

Five thousand tongues applauded as he wiped them on his
shirt;

And while the writhing pitcher ground the ball into his
hip—

Defiance gleamed from Casey's eye—a sneer curled Casey's
lip.

And now the leather-covered sphere came hurtling through
the air,

And Casey stood a-watching it in haughty grandeur there;

Close by the sturdy batsman the ball unheeded sped—

"That hain't my style," said Casey—"Strike one," the Umpire said.

From the bleachers black with people there rose a sullen
roar,

Like the beating of the storm waves on a stern and distant
shore,

"Kill him! kill the Umpire!" shouted some one from the
stand—

And it's likely they'd have done it had not Casey raised his
hand.

With a smile of Christian charity great Casey's visage
  shone,
He stilled the rising tumult and he bade the game go on;
He signalled to the pitcher and again the spheroid flew,
But Casey still ignored it and the Umpire said "Strike two."
"Fraud!" yelled the maddened thousands, and the echo an-
  swered "Fraud."
But one scornful look from Casey and the audience was
  awed;
They saw his face grow stern and cold; they saw his mus-
  cles strain,
And they knew that Casey would not let that ball go by
  again.
The sneer is gone from Casey's lip; his teeth are clenched
  with hate,
He pounds with cruel violence his bat upon the plate;
And now the pitcher holds the ball, and now he lets it go,
And now the air is shattered by the force of Casey's blow.
Oh! somewhere in this favored land the sun is shining
  bright,
The band is playing somewhere, and somewhere hearts
  are light.
And somewhere men are laughing, and somewhere chil-
  dren shout;
But there is no joy in Mudville—mighty Casey has "Struck
  Out."

                              —*Ernest Lawrence Thayer.*

FINNIGIN TO FLANNIGAN

Superintendent wuz Flannigan;
Boss av the siction wuz Finnigin;
Whiniver the kyars got offen the thrack,
An' muddled up things t' th' divil an' back,
Finnigin writ it to Flannigan,
After the wrick wuz all on ag'in;
   That is, this Finnigin
   Repoorted to Flannigan.

Whin Finnigin furst writ to Flannigan,
He writed tin pages—did Finnigin,
An' he tould jist how the smash occurred;
Full minny a tajus, blunderin' wurrd
Did Finnigin write to Flannigan
After the cars had gone on ag'in.
   That wuz how Finnigin
   Repoorted to Flannigan.

Now Flannigan knowed more than Finnigin—
He'd more idjucation, had Flannigan;
An' it wore'm clane an' complately out
To tell what Finnigin writ about
In his writin' to Muster Flannigan.
So he writed back to Finnigin:
   "Don't do sich a sin ag'in;
   Make 'em brief, Finnigin!"

Whin Finnigin got this from Flannigan,
He blushed rosy rid, did Finnigin;
An' he said: "I'll gamble a whole month's pa-ay
That it will be minny an' minny a da-ay
Befoore Sup'rintindint—that's Flannigan—
Gits a whack at this very same sin ag'in.
  From Finnigin to Flannigan
  Repoorts won't be long ag'in."

Wan da-ay, on the siction av Finnigin,
On the road sup'rintinded by Flannigan,
A rail give way on a bit av a curve,
An' some kyars went off as they made the swerve.
"There's nobody hurted," sez Finnigin,
"But repoorts must be made to Flannigan."
  An' he winked at McGorrigan,
  As married a Finnigin.

He wuz shantyin' thin, wuz Finnigin,
As minny a railroader's been ag'in,
An' the shmoky ol' lamp wuz burnin' bright
In Finnigin's shanty all that night—
Bilin' down his repoort, was Finnigin!
An' he writed this here: "Muster Flannigan:
  Off ag'in, on ag'in,
  Gon ag'in —Finnigin."

—Strickland Gillilan.

THE SPELL OF THE YUKON

I wanted the gold, and I sought it;
    I scrabbled and mucked like a slave.
Was it famine or scurvy—I fought it;
    I hurled my youth into a grave.
I wanted the gold, and I got it—
    Came out with a fortune last fall,—
Yet somehow life's not what I thought it,
    And somehow the gold isn't all.

No! There's the land—(have you seen it?)
    It's the cussedest land that I know,
From the big, dizzy mountains that screen it
    To the deep, deathlike valleys below.
Some say God was tired when He made it;
    Some say it's a fine land to shun;
Maybe; but there's some as would trade it
    For no land on earth—and I'm one.

You come to get rich (damned good reason);
    You feel like an exile at first;
You hate it like hell for a season,
    And then you are worse than the worst.
It grips you like some kinds of sinning;
    It twists you from foe to a friend;
It seems it's been since the beginning;
    It seems it will be to the end.

I've stood in some mighty-mouthed hollow
  That's plumb-full of hush to the brim;
I've watched the big, husky sun wallow
  In crimson and gold, and grow dim,
Till the moon set the pearly peaks gleaming,
  And the stars tumbled out, neck and crop;
And I thought that I surely was dreaming,
  With the peace o' the world piled on top.

The summer—no sweeter was ever;
  The sunshiny woods all athrill;
The grayling aleap in the river,
  The bighorn asleep on the hill.
The strong life that never knows harness;
  The wilds where the caribou call;
The freshness, the freedom, the farness—
  O God! how I'm stuck on it all!

The winter! the brightness that blinds you,
  The white land locked tight as a drum,
The cold fear that follows and finds you,
  The silence that bludgeons you dumb.
The snows that are older than history,
  The woods where the weird shadows slant;
The stillness, the moonlight, the mystery,
  I've bade 'em good-by—but I can't.

There's a land where the mountains are nameless,
　And the rivers all run God knows where;
There are lives that are erring and aimless,
　And deaths that just hang by a hair;
There are hardships that nobody reckons;
　There are valleys unpeopled and still;
There's a land—oh, it beckons and beckons,
　And I want to go back—and I will.

They're making my money diminish;
　I'm sick of the taste of champagne.
Thank God! when I'm skinned to a finish
　I'll pike to the Yukon again.
I'll fight—and you bet it's no sham-fight;
　It's hell!—but I've been there before;
And it's better than this by a damsight—
　So me for the Yukon once more.

There's gold, and it's haunting and haunting;
　It's luring me on as of old;
Yet it isn't the gold that I'm wanting
　So much as just finding the gold.
It's the great, big, broad land 'way up yonder,
　It's the forests where silence has lease;
It's the beauty that thrills me with wonder,
　It's the stillness that fills me with peace.

　　　　　　　　　　　—*Robert W. Service.*

I HAVE A RENDEZVOUS WITH DEATH

I have a rendezvous with Death
At some disputed barricade,
When Spring comes back with rustling shade
And apple-blossoms fill the air—
I have a rendezvous with Death
When Spring brings back blue days and fair.

It may be he shall take my hand
And lead me into his dark land
And close my eyes and quench my breath—
It may be I shall pass him still.
I have a rendezvous with Death
On some scarred slope of battered hill
When Spring come round again this year
And the first meadow-flowers appear.

God knows 'twere better to be deep
Pillowed in silk and scented down,
Where Love throbs out in blissful sleep,
Pulse nigh to pulse, and breath to breath,
Where hushed awakenings are dear . . .
But I've a rendezvous with Death
At midnight in some flaming town,
When Spring trips north again this year,
And I to my pledged word am true,
I shall not fail that rendezvous.

—*Alan Seeger.*

THEY WENT FORTH TO BATTLE,
BUT THEY ALWAYS FELL

They went forth to battle, but they always fell;
   Their eyes were fixed above the sullen shields;
Nobly they fought and bravely, but not well,
And sank heart-wounded by a subtle spell.
   They knew not fear that to the foeman yields,
   They were not weak, as one who vainly wields
A futile weapon; yet the sad scrolls tell
How on the hard-fought field they always fell.

It was a secret music that they heard,
   A sad sweet plea for pity and for peace;
And that which pierced the heart was but a word,
Though the white breast was red-lipped where the
      sword
   Pressed a fierce cruel kiss, to put surcease
   On its hot thirst, but drank a hot increase.
Ah, they by some strange troubling doubt were stirred,
And died for hearing what no foeman heard.

They went forth to battle, but they always fell;
   Their might was not the might of lifted spears;
Over the battle-clamor came a spell
Of troubling music, and they fought not well.

Their wreaths are willows and their tribute, tears;
Their names are old sad stories in men's ears;
Yet they shall scatter the red hordes of Hell,
Who went to battle forth and always fell.

—*Shaemas O'Sheel.*

GOD, GIVE US MEN!

God, give us men! A time like this demands
  Strong minds, great hearts, true faith and ready hands;
  Men whom the lust of office does not kill;
Men whom the spoils of office can not buy;
  Men who possess opinions and a will;
Men who have honor; men who will not lie;
Men who can stand before a demagogue
  And damn his treacherous flatteries without winking!
Tall men, sun-crowned, who live above the fog
  In public duty, and in private thinking;
For while the rabble, with their thumb-worn creeds,
Their large professions and their little deeds,
Mingle in selfish strife, lo! Freedom weeps,
Wrong rules the land and waiting Justice sleeps.

—*Josiah Gilbert Holland.*

AMERICA FOR ME

'Tis fine to see the Old World and travel up and down
Among the famous palaces and cities of renown,
To admire the crumbly castles and the statues of the kings
But now I think I've had enough of antiquated things.

So it's home again, and home again, America for me!
My heart is turning home again and there I long to be,
In the land of youth and freedom, beyond the ocean bars,
Where the air is full of sunlight and the flag is full of stars.

Oh, London is a man's town, there's power in the air;
And Paris is a woman's town, with flowers in her hair;
And it's sweet to dream in Venice, and it's great to study
  Rome;
But when it comes to living there is no place like home.

I like the German fir-woods in green battalions drilled;
I like the gardens of Versailles with flashing fountains
  filled;
But, oh, to take your hand, my dear, and ramble for a day
In the friendly western woodland where Nature has her
  sway!

I know that Europe's wonderful, yet something seems to
  lack!

The Past is too much with her, and the people looking
    back.
But the glory of the Present is to make the Future free—
We love our land for what she is and what she is to be.

Oh, it's home again, and home again, America for me!
I want a ship that's westward bound to plough the rolling
    sea,
To the blessed Land of Room Enough, beyond the ocean
    bars,
Where the air is full of sunlight and the flag is full of stars.

—Henry Van Dyke.

FINIS

When the dust of the workshop is still,
The dust of the workman at rest,
May some generous heart find a will
To seek and to treasure his best.

From the splendour of hopes that deceived;
From the wonders he planned to do:
From the glories so nearly achieved;
From the dreams that so nearly came true.

From his struggle to rise above earth
On the pinions that could not fly;
From his sorrows, oh, seek for some worth
To remember the workman by.

If in vain; if Time sweeps all away,
And no laurel from that dust springs;
'Tis enough that a loyal heart say,
"He tried to make beautiful things."

—Eden Phillpotts.

100 Stunts to Add Interest to
Your Meetings

1—"This, I think, is one of the best stunts ever pulled
by our group," says the Secretary of a middle-Western
luncheon club. "We used it in connection with the Red
Cross Flood Relief, but it should work well in securing
funds for any worthy cause.

"A microphone, plainly marked with the initials of
our local broadcasting station, was placed in the room
before the meeting. At five minutes before the hour, our
President called upon the publicity chairman to take over
the meeting. He spoke briefly, stressing the fact that our
club is always ready to help in any crisis, concluding with
the statement that in just about one minute we would
tell the community just what we proposed to do in the
present emergency. At the precise moment, he raised his
hand signifying silence, and made the usual announcement that this program was being broadcast from our
club room, where we were taking contributions for the
Red Cross. Two men were then appointed to take up a
collection. While the plates were being passed, the chairman called upon various members of the club for brief
comment. After several had talked, and the collection
had been taken, a member came in from the rear entrance,

with the end of the microphone cord in his hand saying, 'Fellows, I don't believe this blamed thing was hooked up . . .'

"It was a complete sell-out to everyone but the two or three who were in on the joke. Of course in a stunt of this kind, the setting is the all-important thing. Carefully timed, planned and executed, it is a wow!"

+   +   +

2—Here is a gay little stunt for Ladies' Night, or any informal occasion:

Two captains are appointed (a lady and a gentleman) and each captain chooses another individual. If the captain is a tall man, he chooses a short lady, and vice versa. Then the person chosen chooses another, in the same manner, until six or more have been selected on each side.

Each participant is given a toothpick which he holds in his mouth. The referee then gives each captain a toothpick on which is a candy mint with a hole in the center. The captain is to transfer this mint from his toothpick to that of the person next to him, without either touching it with their hands. That person then transfers the candy to the person next to him in the same manner, and so on, until it eventually returns to the captain. The side first completing a perfect round is the winner. The merriment of this stunt is caused by the difficulty in trying to spear the candy, as it is likely to slip off or break.

+ + +

3—Another stunt of the same general type: Two men are blindfolded and seated one on each side of a card-table. A bowl of dry cereal is placed before each. They are provided with spoons, and are instructed to feed each other. This is a stunt from which the audience gets as much fun as the participants. The laughter often becomes uproarious as the blindfolded persons get the cereal down each other's coat collars, in their ears, or any place other than in the mouth.

+ + +

4—Good-natured stunts which tend to make the tardy member a bit conspicuous are always amusing, and sometimes have a highly beneficial effect in speeding up the chronic laggards. Here is a good one:

A green stove-pipe hat was purchased and turned over to the Sergeant-at-Arms. After the meeting has been called to order, each late-comer is required to wear the green hat until another late-comer arrives. Just before the close of the meeting, the one in possession of the hat pays a forfeit, either singing a solo, or making a small contribution to a club fund for some specified charity. Usually it is a contribution to the fund!

5—The "biographical" stunt is one of the best known ways for the membership to become better acquainted.

There are several variations of this stunt. Use the one which seems best suited to your local situation. One plan is to have a "Biographical" meeting. Announce in advance that a certain number of members will be called upon. Each individual must then be prepared to give his "life history" (talks should be limited to not more than three minutes). If the group is too large to permit every member to speak, the specified number should be drawn by lot, one at a time. A small prize may be presented to the one giving the most creditable performance.

Another plan, and one which has proved very popular, is to have an official "Biographer." This individual should be carefully selected for his ability to talk interestingly. If he possesses a sense of humor, so much the better. It is the duty of this Biographer to interview some member during the course of the week, and present a five-minute biography of that individual at the next meeting. No one knows in advance who is to be selected. A clever biographer will enhance the element of mystery by endeavoring not to reveal the identity of his subject until he is well into the history.

The success of this plan depends largely upon the skill and ability of the one who prepares the biographies. If he is adroit in digging up little-known facts about his subject, weaving in a few anecdotes and good natured jibes, this may readily become the most popular feature of your meeting. Wherever possible, the information should be secured from the subject's wife, business partner, or some other source, so that even the individual himself will not know that his life-story is to be revealed. If this plan is followed, however, some member should be delegated to see that the subject is present, without fail, at the meeting, as much of the success depends upon having the victim on hand to share in the fun.

+ + +

6—One club which recesses during the Summer months, has for many years devoted the first September session to an account of vacation experiences. Members who have visited foreign lands, or out-of-the way regions are called upon to tell, briefly, where they went, what they did and the sights they beheld. The Secretary interviews these members in advance and often suggests questions of general interest which they might care to answer.

+ + +

7—Here's an unusual way to build up interest for an unusual speaker:

When the time has come for the introduction of your speaker, the lights are extinguished. On the table is a photo flash lamp. The first few verses of Genesis are intoned, and at the words "Let there be light," the flash goes and the lights come on. The chairman then ties up with this stunt by saying the speaker will throw as much light on his subject, as we have on the meeting. Needless to say, this has the effect of thoroughly awakening the audience and they listen intently to the message. This stunt should be employed only when you have a magnetic speaker, with an unusual theme—a man whom you know can back up the explosive effect of the flash bulb.

+   +   +

8—An automobile dealer recently conducted a very successful contest stunt, which might have rather wide application. A number of nude manikins—one representing each salesman, is set up in the sales room. Each time a salesman sells a car, an article of apparel is put on his manikin. The contest concluded with a banquet, each salesman attending dressed in the amount of clothing he won during the contest. The tactful dealer, to avoid embarrassment, announced that he would attend the dinner dressed in the same manner as the man who won the fewest number of points.

+   +   +

9—Closely related to the "Biographical" meeting, mentioned previously, is the "Birthplace" stunt. This idea will probably work best in the larger cities, or where your membership comes from various parts of the country. This idea was used with great success by a club in Brooklyn, New York, not long ago.

Each member and guest at the meeting was asked to name the place of his birth; to tell an interesting anecdote associated with his birthplace or his boyhood; to state when he last visited his birthplace, and to give his impressions of it. "Everyone participated readily," says the Secretary, "and this was one of the most interesting and informative meetings we have ever held. Nothing that we had ever done before gave us such an intimate picture of each member."

✦   ✦   ✦

10—The Secretary of a luncheon club in New York state relates this experience:

"At one meeting we had billed a speaker (a member of our Program Committee) who was supposed to give a serious talk on some very profound theme. Just as he was getting well under way, another member burst into the room, selling peanuts and popcorn. He was the type who could carry on in a loud voice, despite the futile efforts of the speaker (who of course was in on the stunt). He sold the bags for a small sum (the proceeds going to a charity in which we are interested).

"No one was permitted to open the bags until the word was given. Then it was found that instead of the supposed wares, each contained a penny "jazz pipe." The pianist then struck up a few chords of a familiar tune and after singing the same through, we incorporated the pipes into the harmony and discovered unsuspected talent amongst our membership.

"We then selected some of the more adroit exhibitionists and formed quartets and double quartets, thus multiplying the fun. The stunt was a big success. Since then we have labeled the pipes with the names of their owners and keep them in a handy place at the hotel for use whenever a session needs a bit of 'pepping up'."

+   +   +

11—The "Straw hat" stunt is a dandy one for early Spring.

Have two men (or import a couple of pretty girls) to pass amongst the membership, recording the head-size of each individual. To the man with the largest head, donate a new straw hat. The man with the smallest head might be given a miniature hat as a consolation prize. This stunt generates a lot of fun and good-natured raillery. You'll have no difficulty in persuading a local merchant to donate a hat, for the publicity value. One of your newspapers will probably be glad to take a photograph of the winner, wearing his new hat, and give you a good story. This means additional publicity for you and the merchant.

12—Here is a stunt that always goes over big at an evening meeting, or some gala occasion:

Obtain from as many members as possible photographs taken in infancy or early childhood. Number these and arrange them on the wall, or on a panel of some sort. Then have the members guess the identity of the persons pictured. The one correctly identifying the largest number may be awarded a prize. An appropriate token might be a coupon, entitling the individual to a free cabinet photograph. Here, again, a local photographer will probably be glad to co-operate with you. The fun can be enhanced if the photographs are secured surreptitiously from some member of the family, instead of directly from the individual.

+ + +

13—A Kiwanis Club put on this "Kiwanis Education" meeting—an idea which might well be adopted by a number of other clubs:

The spokesman appointed two members as captains, and they in turn selected members for a "Kiwanis Bee." The chairman then asked Kiwanis questions of these individuals, beginning with its formation, and coming down to the local club and the classification of its members. A score was kept for each side. This meeting was unusually interesting. It made the members think about the questions, instead of a speaker doing the thinking for them.

+ + +

14—"One of our members who is an amateur photographer," writes a secretary of an Eastern club, "took a number of candid camera shots of various members in informal (and in some cases undignified) moments. Most of the shots were made without the knowledge of the individual. These prints were enlarged and used to brighten a talk on photography which he gave at one of our sessions. The pictures, of course, created a great deal of interest and much merriment. This was voted one of the most popular meetings of the year."

+ + +

15—"Little Known Facts About Well-Known Members" was the way a Nebraska club billed one of its weekly sessions. One member of the club (a newspaper man) spent a great deal of time in ferreting out unusual incidents in the lives of members. An amazing amount of information was gained by talking with wives, friends, acquaintances (in fact, almost everyone except the member himself) and this data, with a bit of humor, was fabricated into a splendid talk that held the interest of everyone present. Naturally, the publicized individuals were even more surprised than anyone else. Some of them are still wondering "where old Bill got all that stuff."

+ + +

16—When a scheduled speaker fails to arrive, and your meeting is in danger of falling flat, why not try the plan of "raffling off" a speaker from your own membership? As the names are drawn, ask the individual to speak for two minutes on a given subject of popular interest.

This idea is subject to many variations. The member, for example, might be asked to give his life history within a specified time limit. Or ask him to tell, in brief, all that he knows of the history or occupation of some other member.

+ + +

17—Another good stunt for a "speakerless" session is the "Inquiring Reporter." Have some member who is experienced in interviewing pass among the membership and propound some question of general interest. Various individuals will be asked to express their views. Better set a strict time limit of one or two minutes, to curb the long-winded lads! Also, be very careful to avoid questions of a too-controversial nature. Naturally, you will want to keep away from religion, politics, and kindred themes. A light, semi-humorous topic is usually best.

+ + +

18—"No Ladies' Night program can be a flop," insists our Kansas City correspondent, "if this feature is introduced as the grand finale. It causes a lot of laughs, and I'll guarantee that the ladies will be craning their necks and probably standing on chairs to watch the stunt.

"Secure from some department store three dummy models, without heads; then make up three separate boxes of ladies' apparel—complete outfits, including corset, lingerie, etc. Announce that a fashion show is to be held and call on three members (good fellows who can take it) to come to the platform. Next, appoint three ladies to act as judges.

"When the men are on the platform, have the models brought out, placing one before each man. Then give each man a box of clothing, and announce that a grand prize will be given to the man who dresses his model the most neatly, and in the shortest time. Impress upon the ladies that it is their duty to choose the best-dressed model.

"When the men open the boxes, the fun begins. Allow about five or ten minutes for dressing the models.

Here's the secret: The only thing necessary to have the 'best dressed' model is to put the dress on neatly. However, the men will invariably try to put on everything.

"After the best-dressed model is chosen, present the winner with a fashion magazine, as a 'grand prize'." Our correspondent further states that he has put on this stunt at least a dozen times with huge success.

+ + +

19—Here is an idea that, in one club at least, helped to break up the tendency of members to gather in small groups or cliques, the same fellows sitting week after week at a certain table. Each seat at the various tables was numbered and luncheon tickets bore corresponding numbers. The members were then asked to find their places by number. This insured practically a complete New Deal, and resulted in some new companionships being formed, which bore fruit at future meetings. This is recommended as an occasional "get acquainted" stunt, rather than as a rigid rule to be enforced at all meetings.

+ + +

20—Here's one of those "catch" stunts, which always get a meeting off to a good start. It works best to "break the ice" with a group of comparative strangers. Especially good for church meetings:

The chairman suggests that a "stretch" would do us all good, and then proceeds with some informal calesthenics, each action performed at a sharp command. Then, very quickly, the chairman calls, "Shake hands with the fellow behind you!" All turn to shake—and there is, of course, a vast expanse of back, since the other fellow, too, has turned. Everyone is "taken in," and a hearty laugh ensues.

It's a honey, if worked quickly—and after the proper build-up.

+   +   +

21—And here is another one that is good for an evening frolic. It has especially fine possibilities for a men's church group, since some of the more dignified members may become a little apprehensive during the preliminaries—and this adds to the fun.

Announce a "boxing match," choosing two contestants, their seconds and a referee. An improvised "ring" may be formed of rope, with four men to hold the corners. Give the two contestants fighting names, and work up a lot of excitement with the ballyhoo. Put a pair of boxing gloves on each contestant, making certain that every detail is conducted according to "regulations."

Then the fun begins! Just when the crowd is expecting some action, bring out the boards of two boxes that have been knocked down; give each man a hammer and the same number of nails. The first to reconstruct his box, without removing the gloves, wins. If you wish, the contest may be conducted by "rounds" with an official time-keeper. Men enjoy this stunt. You can have a lot of fun with it.

+ + +

22—We all know that the success of a membership drive depends largely upon arousing a spirit of good-natured rivalry. And it has been pretty well demonstrated that men will work harder to avoid a penalty, or a conspicuous "booby" than they will to attain a prize.

Here is a stunt tried out by an Illinois club. The secretary says, "It really worked!"

In launching a membership drive, the committee decided, as a preliminary, to induct a mascot into the organization. It was agreed that this should be a goat. Accordingly, a black angora goat was secured, and escorted with great secrecy to the hotel where meetings were held.

Following a brief talk in which the virtues of this proposed "honorary member" were exploited, this "outstanding personality" was pushed from a rear entrance into the meeting room.

Then the committee presented its plan. The campaign was to last four weeks, and the club was divided into four teams. Each week the low team was obliged to take

the goat, keep him for a week, and escort him to the
next meeting. This resulted in some tall hustling for
members. Nobody wanted that goat the first week—and
certainly not for *two* weeks!

+ + +

23—In round table discussions, have each one in attendance given a number. Duplicate numbers are
drawn from a hat, one by one, to select speakers in the
discussions. Introductions are made *before* the numbers
are drawn. The humor thus injected leavens the usual
seriousness of the discussion.

+ + +

24—Why not try a Dunking party sometime when
doughnuts are on the menu? A good deal of fun may
be had by passing around a leaflet, "Rules and Regulations on Dunking." Briefly, here are the rules:

1—Tuck a nice, clean napkin around your neck.

2—Pick up a doughnut daintily with the thumb and
first finger only. The other three fingers must point
outward.

3—Dip the doughnut gently into the milk, cocoa or
coffee.

4—Move the dougtnut slowly back and forth in the cup
to help it absorb as much as it can.

5—Remove the doughnut and hold it above the cup until
all the extra drops have dripped back.

6—Bite off the wet portion and repeat the above process until there are no more doughnuts left.

These leaflets on Dunking (with clever illustrations) are put out by the Kresge stores.

+ + +

25—This stunt threatened momentarily to wreck the Kiwanis club where it was first tried out. A member obtained the floor and pointed out that while the club had done much in support of the City Hospital, an opportunity had now come for further service. He then introduced the Superintending Nurse of the hospital, and asked her to explain.

The nurse, after extending her appreciation for all that the club had done, said that an orphan baby was in their care and suggested that the club might find a home for it. At this point, a member suggested that a drawing be made, the fifth name out should be the Kiwanian to take this orphan baby. Despite outraged protests from the membership, the officers proceeded with the lottery, while a sudden stillness came over the room, as each man anticipated the responsibility that might soon be his. The name drawn was that of a member who had five or six children. The nurse then explained that the baby was in the hotel at that time, and would be brought in. A member was delegated to accompany her, as she went to

bring it in. They returned with a crib, which turned out
to contain a little pig, wrapped up in the bedding.

+ + +

26—Here's a good stunt to get the boys to know each
other. You might use it every once in a while:

Call on a member to introduce as many members as
he can, calling each by his first and last name, and giving
the business in which he is engaged. When the first man
fails, call on the member he couldn't name to continue,
and so on, until the entire membership has been introduced. Every member who fails is fined a dime.

+ + +

27—This stunt may be used for an initiation party, or
for any general jollification:

The required props are two clown suits—extra large
and baggy—and about thirty small rubber balloons. Blindfold or mask the two candidates, dress them in the suits
and stuff as many of the inflated balloons as you can in
legs, arms and body of the suits. Have four members
form an arena about sixteen feet square, by holding a
heavy rope taut.

The master of ceremonies introduces the contestants
in the Great Blindfolded Wrestling Match, giving the
participants any instructions he may think necessary. The

candidates are then led to the arena, and asked to climb into the ring. Every fall and roll will start the balloons popping. This stunt creates a lot of good laughs.

+ + +

28—Here's a slight variation of the fake radio broadcast.

Borrow a standard microphone from a local radio station. An hour or so before program time, telephone several outstanding members of the club, informing them that broadcasting equipment has been obtained for the meeting. Ask each man to be prepared to deliver a five-minute speech on a specified subject.

Be careful not to state directly that the program is going on the air, but of course that is the impression your selected members will get. Most of them will take the matter quite seriously, and make elaborate preparations for the broadcast. At the conclusion, the presiding officer may regretfully announce that someone has neglected to connect the microphone, so of course the splendid speeches were not carried out over the ether waves as intended. The speakers will probably join in the general laughter.

+ + +

29—This dog-calling stunt was originated by a Kansas Club, and we think it has a lot of possibilities.

Select as participants in this stunt three members of the club who own dogs, and who are known to take a personal interest in their respective canine friends. Buy three cans of dog food (the only money expense necessary.) Designate your actors as A, B and C. Take the wife of C into your confidence and by pre-arrangement bring the dog belonging to C to the meeting well ahead of the time set, and secrete the animal so that it will easily be available at the proper time. Have an attendant in charge of the dog at all times, to prevent any slip-up.

The master of ceremonies now asks A to come forward. He is asked if he owns a dog; the name, breed, sex, etc. Next, A is asked to give an accurate imitation of the way in which he calls his dog when he reaches home in the evening. (Some call by name, but most men use a peculiar whistle). This performance always gets a good laugh from the audience. As a reward for a good job of dog-calling, A is given a can of dog food.

B is then put through the same quiz, and usually tries to outdo A. He also is rewarded with a can of dog food. Now comes C's turn. He is, of course, unaware that his dog has been brought into an adjoining room. The master of ceremonies keeps up a constant chatter to hold C's attention to the matter at hand, and as he goes into action with a rousing call for his purp, the animal is unleashed and makes a dash for the front to greet his surprised master. C is now stuck, with his dog at his heels, for the remainder of the evening.

+   +   +

30—This stunt might work well in a situation where there is keen rivalry between two nearby towns. It was originated at a joint meeting of the Minneapolis and St. Paul Lions clubs. At a fun night, with about 150 men present from both clubs, a presiding officer arose and said that there was one matter of serious business to be discussed. He then read what purported to be a telegram from the Secretary General of Lions International, suggesting that in order to promote a kindlier feeling in the two towns, International would like to have these clubs merge into a single unit, holding meetings each week at some convenient spot.

A committee was finally appointed, after many remarks from the members. The veteran secretary of the St. Paul club remarked very touchingly that he probably would lose his job, which had been keeping him alive during the depression, if the merger became effective. Most of the membership was completely "taken in" until the committee, meeting separately, reported to the group. The men on the committee expressed themselves favorably on the matter of a merger, and suggested that meetings be held in Murphy's Livery Stable, situated close to the line. Then, of course, the boys saw it was all a hoax, and everyone present had a good laugh.

+ + +

31—Every club can ring many variations on the old "get acquainted" stunt. Here's one way it might be done:

Have two sets of numbers prepared, covering the membership of the club. Two members pass around the tables, starting at opposite ends, giving each man a number on a slip of paper. At a specified time, the presiding officer asks members holding Number 1 to stand. When these two members stand, each is asked to tell the name of the other, and his business. If a member fails to answer correctly, he is fined according to the rules of the club. The officer then proceeds with Number 2, and so on, until all have responded.

+ + +

32—Still another "get acquainted" plan:

Call upon one member at each table to name every individual at that table. For each error, he pays a small fine or forfeit. This becomes a lesson to the member, and from that time on he makes it his business to become better acquainted with those about him.

33—We've already discussed the fake radio program from several angles, but the "distant city" broadcast is still another angle which holds some possibilities. The Chairman announces that the club is to hear a program of club members from an out-of-town station, and that the entertainment will come on at a specified time, over a radio, especially installed for the purpose.

Of course the committee in charge has the program arranged, with music, singing and humorous features. Those taking part, are stationed in another room of the building, with microphone in that room, connected to the luncheon room where a loud-speaker is installed.

At the specified time, the program begins. Voices of well-known members are heard, but the group, of course, is not aware that these persons are in the same building. Members participating in the program are, of course, not to be seen by anyone in the audience until after the program, when the hoax may be revealed.

+ + +

34—The Indianapolis Kiwanis Club recently held an unusual celebration in honor of a past president who was ill and had been confined to his home for several weeks. Arrangements were made to broadcast the program over a local radio station, and the honored officer was thus permitted to "listen in" on a program which he could not attend in person.

The meeting was presided over by the senior past president. The Mayor, President of the Chamber of Commerce, and other prominent citizens spoke briefly of the fine service and excellent civic spirit which this gentleman had always shown. The meeting was well attended, and of course received good publicity in the local newspapers.

+ + +

35—This perhaps could not be classified as a stunt, but it is a first-class plan adopted by a number of clubs. In effect, it is a method of paying annual dues on the installment plan.

A small sum (usually about 25 cents) is added to the price of the luncheon. Thus, if the hotel charges 50 cents for the meal, the member pays 75 cents for his ticket; if the luncheon charge is 75 cents, he pays one dollar. The extra sum goes toward the payment of dues.

The advantages of this plan are evident. The treasury has a continuous flow of money, and even those members who may be a bit hard pressed scarcely miss the small weekly contributions. They no longer face the bugaboo of an annual or semi-annual bill.

Weekly payments may be set up on a basis so that even though a member misses a few meetings, he still will have his bill paid by the end of the year; or you can arrange so that if a member is absent one week, he pays

double the next time. Of course a record must be kept
of each man's payments. When he has paid in a sum
equal to his annual dues, he will not be asked for any
further contributions until the beginning of a new term.

+ + +

36—To find a stunt that is amusing, and at the same
time a good money-raiser is not a simple matter. The
Taunton, Massachusetts Lions Club recently found something that answered this description—a turtle race. A
fairly large circle was drawn on the floor, and four
turtles (each with a different color spot on his back)
were placed in the ring. Tickets were sold on the race,
the winner receiving some toy. Toys were later donated
to children. Receipts were not large—only about $15.00
—but it was all clear profit, and the gang had a hilarious
time.

+ + +

37—In all probability, you can induce a local theatre
or motion picture house to contribute a pair of tickets
each week, to be given as an attendance prize. Have the
membership draw numbers from a hat, the lucky number, of course, to get the complimentary tickets. If maintained regularly, this can become quite an institution in
the club, and will build a great deal of good-will for the
theatre.

38—"Our club has used successfully the initiation of a father, upon the arrival of a new baby," says a Mississippi club secretary. "At some appointed time during the meeting, the new father is blindfolded, and asked to submit to an initiation into the Proud Fathers of America. The conductor of the stunt makes appropriate remarks as to the distinction which the father has brought to himself and to the club. Then the victim's finger prints are taken for the organization. This is done by placing both hands in soft fresh mustard, spread on a platter. The hands are then pressed firmly down on a white napkin, spread on the table. The blindfold is removed, and the prints exhibited to the audience.

"As a concluding feature, the conductor presents the initiate with the insignia of the order, either a necklace made of safety pins, or a table napkin folded diaperlike and hung around his neck."

+ + +

39—Here is a Kiwanis stunt with a five-fold purpose: (1) to stimulate regular attendance; (2) to increase each member's personal acquaintance with other members; (3) to increase the knowledge of the members of Kiwanis and its activities; (4) to cause members to sit at different tables each week, thus breaking up small cliques; and (5) to provide some good fun for all.

This plan was tried out in a club of 110 members. In a weekly letter to the membership was included two or three questions pertaining to Kiwanis, giving each member an opportunity to learn the answers to these questions before the next meeting. Each member's name is placed on a card, and there is a drawing every week for an attendance prize of $1.00. However, before the lucky member can claim his dollar bill, he must overcome the following hazards:

(1) Did he sit at the same table last week? (If so, he is not eligible for the prize.)

(2) Can he answer the questions in the last Kiwanis letter? (If he fails, he is not eligible for the prize.)

(3) Can he give the first and last names of all Kiwanians at his table? (If he fails, he is not eligible for the prize.)

If the member whose name is drawn is not able to qualify on all counts, the dollar is added to the "kitty" until claimed by an eligible member. At times, we are told, the fund has totaled as much as $6.00 or $8.00.

+   +   +

40—As a sequel, in a club where the foregoing plan proved highly successful, the Kiwanis Education Committee, at a meeting for which it was responsible, engendered some good fun with this program:

Unexpectedly, the chairman of the committee asked all officers, directors and past presidents of the club to stand. He then proceeded to ask questions pertaining to Kiwanis, its organization and activities. When an individual "missed" on a question, he was asked to sit down. In this manner, the chairman "spelled down" every past president, director and officer of the club, to the great amusement of all members, particularly those who had previously failed to receive an attendance prize because of failure to answer questions on Kiwanis.

+ + +

41—An original stunt which caused complete bewilderment at a certain luncheon club, was the reading of the *middle name* only of each member present. When a member failed to recognize his name, his identity was revealed, and he was fined.

+ + +

42—This hoax letter stunt is an ideal feature to present at a meeting where your speaker is a member of the Better Business Bureau, or some organization devoted to exposing slick schemes and sharp practices.

The chairman of the meeting reads a letter by some prominent citizen, addressed to an outside organization, supporting a worthwhile project, or protesting some proposed activity. A postscript on the letter states that on the attached sheets are found the names of prominent business men of the locality who endorse the subject matter of the letter.

This letter is supposed to circulate among the men at tables, while the meeting is in progress. Instead, another letter, with the letter part folded over and pinned down, is substituted. Sheep-like, the men proceed to sign their names without investigation.

The letter actually used, asks for a $50.00 donation by each signer, for some utterly foolish project. When it has gone the rounds, it is returned to the presiding officer, who totals up the amount and reveals to the men what they have pledged. No one has read the letter, and you certainly have a group of foolish-looking fellows when the announcement is made.

This stunt was pulled on sixty men at a luncheon, and worked without a hitch.

+ + +

43—At your next Past President's Day, you can engender a lot of fun by having these gentlemen appear with beards and costumes of thirty years ago. They should carry canes and convey, by stooped shoulders and otherwise, an air of age and decrepitude.

+ + +

44—Here's an idea that was carried out by one club on Lincoln's birthday. It would work equally well in celebrating the birthday of any national hero, or perhaps some renowned local character. This club announced in its weekly club letter that each member should come prepared to give the story or incident in Lincoln's life that had made the most lasting impression upon him. The meeting was quite successful, and the result was a number of interesting stories, many of which were new to a majority of the members.

+ + +

45—For an evening's frolic, it's hard to beat a Salmagundi Party. The idea here is to provide a series of tables, with a different game or stunt at each table. The winners at one table, progress to the next. A variety of games can be readily obtained. Here are a few stunts that might go well: Piling matches on top of a narrow-neck bottle, all matches falling off to be counted against the couple that causes them to fall; stringing beads; playing dominoes; making words out of the letters in the club president's name. A time limit is set for each stunt. After time is called, each adds his score, or determines his standing, and winners move. This idea works better at a party where ladies are present.

+ + +

46—In installing seven new officers, one club lined up the men according to their rank, and had them handcuffed together by a local policeman. A convict cap, made of paper was placed on each head. A placard was then attached to each individual, reading, "Sentenced to Serve—Kiwanis Club for One Year." Under each placard was placed the convict's serial number.

The "gang" was then marched into the meeting room by the policeman. Each man was charged with the duties of his office by the judge. At the close of the meeting, the policeman disappeared with the only keys to the handcuffs. The seven men had a pleasant hour together —and sore wrists—by the time the policeman was found.

+ + +

47—"How did you get into your present vocation?" is a theme rich in possibilities for a club session. Have five club members take not to exceed five minutes each to sketch the route which led up to their present position in life. Then have some humorous member, with a gift of banter, to comment on the stories, taking up each man's talk in turn. This not only gives an insight on your fellow members, but is excellent entertainment, especially if the closing comment is well handled.

+ + +

48—Club singing is, of course, a rather common practice. Here, however, is a variation that may add to the interest—and to the fun. Take one selection—Clementine, for example—and go through all of the verses, with a different member designated on the spur of the moment to get up and sing the verse, after which all join in the chorus. The song-leader picks out the soloist in each case.

+ + +

49—A great many clubs, as you probably know, have abolished the practice of members calling· each other "Mister." Anyone who addresses anyone else as "Mister," or refers to another member, using that term, is fined ten cents, which goes into the crippled children's fund.

+ + +

50—There is, of course, nothing new in the attendance prize idea, but here is an unusual method developed by one club in determining the winner. Each week a different member (determined in alphabetical order) brings an attendance prize, valued at about $1.00. The drawing is from the attendance slips of the preceding week. In a club of 50, no man gives more than one attendance prize in a year. Five names are drawn from the lot. All five stand up. Then drawings are made from those five. As each of the first four names is called, the crowd yells "Sit down!" The last man up, of course, wins the prize.

51—Most club members are married. They have wedding anniversaries. The secretary of one club has secured a list of these anniversaries. On the meeting date nearest each anniversary, he orders a rose which is given to the man to take home to his wife. This stunt may also be used for the birthday of the member.

+ + +

52—At a Ladies Night why shouldn't the ladies themselves provide some of the entertainment? That, at least, was the way one group reasoned. At a Kiwanis festivity eight wives got together and put on a black-face minstrel show, lasting about an hour. They offered the traditional jokes of the end-men, using of course the names of club members and their wives.

+ + +

53—Here are a couple of stunts for an April Fool meeting: Handle the attendance prize drawing as is usual in your club. When the winner has been determined, ask him to come forward. As he approaches, the presiding officer stammers apologetically that a mistake has been made. The attendance prize is for the *next* meeting. Have several in the audience primed to cry "April fool!"

Another plan is to secure a large bottle, fill it with sarsaparilla or some non-staining liquid. The bottle should be wrapped. Hold the drawing as usual. When the presiding officer is about to hand the bottle to the winner, he manages to drop it on the floor. The bottle breaks with a resulting howl from the audience.

+ + +

54—If you want to get a rough idea of the conditions that probably prevailed in building the Tower of Babel, try this: Have three members planted in different parts of the room. On a pre-arranged signal, the three men rise with one accord and begin talking at once, each on a different subject. This is a good stunt, but should not be prolonged. Two minutes will extract the essence of the fun. Better stage a dress rehearsal and check carefully on the timing.

+ + +

55—Still another one to harass the late-comer: Everyone coming in after the session starts is greeted by the ringing of a cow-bell—and compelled to drop a dime in the bank.

+ + +

56—"Who shall give the next attendance prize?" has been solved by one club in this satisfactory manner: Attendance slips are put into the hat. The first drawn is discarded; the second, likewise; the third name drawn is the winner and the fourth, the donor of a prize for the next meeting.

+ + +

57—Here's a recipe for raising a fund easily and quickly: Raffle off a "Gentleman's Hope Chest" (a suitcase containing fine liquors).

+ + +

58—This, insists the perpetrator, is good for a lot of laughs. We suggest, however, that the man who is putting on the stunt, should make certain that his accident insurance premiums are fully paid up:

Some member is called upon to raise $5.00 or $10.00 quickly. He then (pre-arranged) collects several other members' hats, along with a couple of old hats and raffles them off.

When the hat is raffled, the owner's name is, of course, announced.

If the bidding lags a bit, the auctioneer takes one of the old hats, in apparent disgust, and tears it up. This may be done a second time with another old hat. From this point on, you may be sure, the bidding will jump in a hurry.

+ + +

59—In a large middle western city, the Lions Club, in co-operation with the aviation committee of the Chamber of Commerce, arranged a special meeting to honor two local aviation pilots and a stewardess all of whom had flown more than 150,000 miles in the service of one of the leading commercial airlines. Special guests were the mayor, the governor of the state and the superintendent of the municipal airport.

The meeting aroused a great deal of interest, and was pronounced a decided success by all concerned.

+   +   +

60—For a number of years a leading luncheon club in a fair-sized city has made it a practice to select each year an outstanding man or woman who, in the judgment of an appointed committee has rendered the most constructive and unselfish service to the community in the preceding twelve months. This individual is then honored at a special luncheon meeting, at which the most prominent and influential persons in town are invited guests. This results, of course, in a great deal of excellent publicity for the club.

+   +   +

61—The "drafted" quartet is an idea that often puts new life into your song period. There are a number of ways in which individuals may be selected at random to form impromptu quartets. One club works it this way: Small cards or slips of paper are provided in sufficient number to allow one for each person present. On one of the cards, the letter "S" is written, on another "I"; a third bears the letter "N" and a fourth "G." Individuals who draw these letters, spelling the word "SING" must arrange themselves around the piano and render a popular selection. It is a rule of the club that no one drafted in this manner can refuse to participate. Some mighty funny combinations will turn up, and this of course adds to the general hilarity.

+ + +

62—One club secretary reports great success with an impromptu "ladies day." They worked it this way: By previous engagement, the wife of one of the officers (a rather timid chap) just "happened" to be in the lobby of the hotel a few minutes before the time appointed for the meeting. She suggested that it might be a nice idea to "have lunch with the men"—a suggestion which, needless to say, her horrified husband promptly vetoed. Ladies, he insisted, were invited only on special occasions. But the wife would not be so easily put off. She insisted, much to her husband's embarrassment. About that time, she spied the wife of another member, and rushed over to extend an invitation to her. Other women continued to arrive, by twos and threes, and it was some time before it dawned upon the members that the whole thing was a "plant." Special entertainment had been provided, and it turned out to be a very enjoyable occasion.

63—Why not try a "What This Town Needs . . ." meeting? This may be a pre-arranged affair, with selected speakers; or it may be conducted in the manner of an open forum, with every man privileged to speak his mind. If you wish, give a prize for the most constructive suggestion.

+ + +

64—"Ours is one of the oldest luncheon clubs in the city," writes a secretary, "and on the occasion of the twenty-fifth anniversary of our founding, we decided to honor our oldest member (in point of service). A special meeting was arranged in his honor, and we presented him with a scroll, bearing the signatures of every member of the club. Several old-timers talked on the early history and activities of the club, concluding of course with a talk by our honor guest. It was a fine meeting, and we got a lot of first-rate publicity in the papers."

+ + +

65—At the last meeting of the year, one club decided to turn the spotlight on new members inducted during the previous twelve months. Without saying anything to these newcomers, the secretary ordered a sufficient number of very ornate "baby bonnets" made up, of course, in adult sizes. As the "babies" arrived they were ushered into an adjoining room. A bonnet was put on each man, with elaborate bow tied under the chin. Lollipops of varying colors were provided, and the youngsters escorted to a table reserved for them. As an added feature, the club wit recited nursery rhymes, bringing in the names and occupations of the new members.

+ + +

66—During Boy Scout week, a club in New England invited a local Boy Scout troop to meet with them. The boys, on this occasion, also served as officers of the club, and conducted the meeting. A scout patrol performed a number of stunts, such as tying knots, first-aid, etc. Club members were then singled out and asked to duplicate the stunts. Their clumsy efforts occasioned much merriment. A serious talk by the Scoutmaster concluded the program.

+ + +

67—A "What I would do if I had your job" program is an idea that can be adopted by almost any club. Work it this way: Select five men from your group who are known to be pretty good impromptu speakers. Have each draw from the hat a card on which is written the name and business of some other member of the club. The speaker must then tell, in not more than five minutes, how he would handle that particular situation. Have the cards drawn one at a time, so that the speaker has absolutely no time for meditation. You may get some constructive suggestions of real value. And certainly you'll have a lot of fun. At one session where this stunt was tried, a preacher kept everyone in an uproar by telling facetiously how he would conduct a plumbing business, and the manager of a public utility got an idea from a grocer which he declared was worth the price of a year's dues.

+ + +

68—An idea, somewhat related to the foregoing, is a session at which members tell why they are glad they do not have So-and-So's job. One man, for example may picture the calamity that would have prevailed had he chanced to take up barbering. Another may suggest that his idea of a job not to have is that of information clerk in a railway station, and so on.

+ + +

69—"Notables I have known" was an idea that took hold in one club. It developed that a surprising number of the members had known, intimately or casually, individuals of more or less prominence. Many interesting anecdotes were related. One man in the group had gone to school with a President of the United States. Another had known a celebrated prize fighter in the years before he attained the limelight. Authors, politicians, and inventors were mentioned, also.

In putting on a stunt of this kind it probably would be well to talk the idea over with a few members, and have one or two primed to start the ball rolling. These stories will suggest individuals and incidents to others, and soon several will be eager to speak.

+ + +

70—This will keep them occupied at an evening party:

Have each member write out some question connected with his occupation. Thus, a lawyer might inquire: "What is the exact definition of habeas corpus?" A doctor asks: "What is a spatula?" A tailor: "How many yards of material in an average man's 3-piece suit?"

List all of these questions on a sheet of paper, provide a copy for each person present, and set them to work. Prizes, of course, for the most accurate answers.

+ + +

71—The "balloon fight" is an old stunt, but still good for many a laugh at an informal gathering. Let two captains "choose up" from the membership—four to six men on a side. Fasten an inflated balloon to the ankle of each contestant. Give the signal, and turn them loose. Each side tries to burst the balloons of their opponents.

Since feet only may be used, a general tangle ensues. Works well at a picnic or open-air meeting.

+ + +

72—The "mute guest" is one of the oldest of our group gags, but though threadbare, may still be quite effective on occasion. Have some member present a guest (a stranger to the others, of course) as a mute. The guest acknowledges introductions with a smile; converses with his host in sign language, or writes messages on a scratch pad. At an opportune time have the "mute" astonish everyone with some explosive comment.

+ + +

73—The problem of selecting delegates to attend a convention is sometimes a rather ticklish one. Perhaps only one or two men from the group can attend, yet all contribute to the fund. To avoid any possibility of favoritism, why not have a jackpot drawing? Sometime prior to the convention, set up a jackpot to which all contribute equally—a specified sum each week. Then, when convention time arrives, put all names in a hat and draw for the winner, who gets the fund, on condition, of course, that he agrees to attend the convention as a delegate of the club. This provision is necessary in order to prevent possible complications if the member finds at the last moment that he cannot make the trip. In that case, a second drawing must be held, to make certain that the money goes for the purpose intended.

+ + +

74—If you are fortunate enough to be situated in a city with a good municipal airport, served by one of the major airlines, you should have little difficulty in getting an executive of the airline to address your group. This new industry is eager for favorable publicity. As an added feature, they might even be willing to award a round-trip airplane ticket to some nearby metropolis. This could be given as an attendance prize, and will stir up a great deal of interest in the meeting, insuring a big turn-out.

+ + +

75—A luncheon club located in a city which has a large hosiery mill, arranged an unusual feature for their annual Ladies' Day program. Following the club luncheon, the ladies were transported to the hosiery plant for a tour of inspection. Upon arriving at the plant, each lady gave her measurements for a pair of hose. Two hours later, upon departing, the hose were presented to her. They were manufactured to her order during the interval. A mending kit and a bottle of perfume also were included as favors.

This is an idea which is subject to many variations. In almost every city there is some large manufacturing plant that would be only too glad to act as host to a group of ladies, entertaining them and distributing samples of the product as souvenirs.

+ + +

76—Here's a stunt to try when the ladies are present: A Southern club had a lot of fun with it, so the secretary reports. Wives of the members were masked and grouped in an adjoining room. The doors to this room were then opened and the club members instructed to find their wives and take them in to dinner. Perhaps the boys didn't put their hearts into the hunt, for strangely enough almost every man had another member's wife!

+ + +

77—If you identify members by badges, try withholding these at some meeting. Then test the memory of your group by having each member write down the name and classification of every other member present. For this purpose, have a sheet of paper and pencil at each place. Collect these sheets before the program begins, and have two officers grade them, deducting a point for each error in name or classification. At the conclusion of the meeting announce the winner and give his score. Winner may receive a small prize or a free meal.

78—Why not make a special effort now and then to have your attendance or booster prizes tie in with the occasion or the season? At Thanksgiving, for example, you might give a turkey instead of the usual cigarettes, books, letter files, etc.

+ + +

79—Who can think of the largest number of slang words?

Try it out at an evening frolic. Give each contestant a sheet of paper and pencil. Set a time limit—say five minutes. Announce that a prize will be given, but do not specify what it is, or the conditions. When the list has been handed in and duly graded, have some individual who can assume a pompous attitude arise and talk for a few moments, deploring the prevalence of slang, as indicated by the entries, and in conclusion *award the prize to the individual who has turned in the smallest number of slang terms.*

This stunt will work well anywhere, but is especially good for a church or Sunday School group.

+ + +

80—A "Tall Tales" session always goes well in a small, informal group. This may be impromptu, or members may be instructed in advance to come prepared to tell some outlandish tale. The winner may be designated the Biggest Liar in the club, and given a medal or certificate to this effect.

+   +   +

81—Stage a "Safety" meeting in co-operation with your local traffic officers. You should have no difficulty in getting someone from the Police Department who can give an interesting and instructive talk on safe driving. As an added feature, you might select members to talk on "My Narrowest Escape—And What It Taught Me." Local papers will be glad to play up the meeting.

+   +   +

82—Next time you select a few men from your group to be honored as old-timers, instead of scattering them throughout the room, have them seated in one long column, directly below the head table. Prior to the introduction, have each man speedily stick a set of long whiskers on his chin.

+   +   +

83—If you are located in a city of more than 100,000 population it is probable that you have several travel agencies, maintained independently or functioning as departments of local banks. Very often these agencies will be able to get short films for you on regions of special interest. Speakers, too, are generally available.

Railroads are another good source of travel films. The Northern roads will show pictures of Winter sports, in season; the Western roads are glad to present films of Yellowstone, Grand Canyon, etc. These are interesting to your members, and there is usually no cost.

+ + +

84—A "Mystery Auction" is one of the oldest meth-- ods of raising money—and still one of the best. Have members ransack attic and basement for small miscel- laneous articles that are no longer of value to them. Bring these to a central spot for auction. To enhance the interest, have the articles wrapped attractively, so that the buyer will have no idea what he is getting. In addi- tion to the usual collection of coal-oil lamps and hand- embroidered what-nots should be a few items of real worth. All merchandise should be unwrapped on the spot. This should result in much hilarity, and quite a bit of trading on the side.

A good way for a church or social organization to raise a neat sum of money, without risk or investment.

+ + +

85—If yours is a fairly large club, why not arrange with some competent instructor to give a course of les- sons in public speaking on one or two evenings a week, making up a class exclusively of club members? A num-

ber will join who might otherwise hesitate. When the
class "graduates," after a period of two or three months,
you can have them take over a meeting and demonstrate
what they have learned.

+   +   +

86—Some years ago, a congenial group in a certain
luncheon club reflected that since they ate luncheon
downtown each day, it might be pleasant to eat together
on occasions other than the regular luncheon day. The
hotel was glad to set aside a table in the dining room,
exclusively for club members. Announcement was made
at a regular meeting that all members, and their guests
would be welcomed. Now, fifteen to twenty club members may be found at this table every noon (except, of
course, the day reserved for regular meetings). It has had
a splendid effect in bringing the men closer together.

+   +   +

87—Have you a club bulletin board? An Ohio club
installed one about a year ago. At first members were
inclined to treat the idea a bit facetiously, but now it has
become a valuable means of imparting information. If
member A is looking for a bright young girl to do general office work, he announces the fact in a brief bulletin.
Member B has two sons who are looking for employ-
ment during the Summer months. Again the bulletin

board is used. Recently, a member wanted to sell a few pieces of antique furniture that had belonged to his father. He described the offering briefly in a bulletin, and by the following noon had received three telephone calls.

+ + +

88—A number of excellent programs may be built around films distributed by various federal agencies. In the United States these films are available, without charge, to any organization that will pay transportation cost to and from Washington. The Department of Agriculture has perhaps the largest selection of motion pictures. However, the Navy, the Bureau of Reclamation, the National Park Service and other departments also have interesting subjects to offer.

With keen interest in health now evident, a timely program might well be worked out with films furnished by the U. S. Public Health Service.

The U. S. Office of Education, Washington, D. C., has compiled a list of all Government films, and a copy of this list will be furnished free of charge, on request.

+ + +

89—Few persons in the larger communities know very much about the early history of the city in which they reside. Why not check up, find the date of your city charter; learn something of its early history and set

aside one program annually to honor the birthday of
your city? Have some old inhabitant to talk on early
events and old landmarks; invite the mayor and members of the city council as your special guests. A meeting
of this type should be assured of excellent publicity.

+ + +

90—This stunt caused a lot of amusement in the club
where it was tried out:

An alarm clock was set to go off within a few minutes
—the exact time was not announced—and the clock was
then passed from member to member. The man who
chanced to hold the clock as the alarm sounded, was required to make a three-minute impromptu speech. The
excitement and hilarity will run high, as of course each
member is anxious to get rid of the clock as quickly as
possible when it is passed to him.

+ + +

91—Try this stunt on a member who shows up after
an absence of several weeks: Put him into a regular convict suit, and proceed to hold a mock trial. All court
officers are appointed by the Stunts committee. This can
be enlarged upon and made the occasion of a good deal
of merriment.

92—Here's a clever little stunt for an evening party:

Obtain a plank ten or twelve feet long, place it on the floor elevating one end about eight or ten inches. Bring a blindfold victim (who, of course, has not seen the plank) and inform him that, as a result of some misdemeanor he will be compelled to "walk the plank." He is led to the plank, with one man on each side. His hands are placed on the shoulders of these men. As he walks, the men gradually lower themselves, giving the walker the impression of steadily climbing to a great height. At the end of the plank someone lying on the floor hands up an open umbrella to serve as a parachute. The blindfolded individual is then commanded to jump. You can imagine his surprise when he discovers that he has descended only a few inches instead of several feet.

+ + +

93—Why not arrange an exchange program with some club in a neighboring city? Undoubtedly you have sufficient talent in your organization to put on a sure-fire program. Tell this neighbor club that your members will take over one of their meetings, providing speaker and entertainment features if they will do the same for you. Both programs are likely to be first class as neither club will want to be "shown up" by the other.

94—If yours is a craft club (such as Advertising, Traffic, Business Correspondence, or the like) you might very profitably make some effort to train or enlighten the younger generation. An Advertising club, for example, might sponsor a short course in advertising for high school and college students who have special interest in the subject. The course, naturally, could not assume to make the student an expert in a few evenings, but it could at least implant a few fundamentals, and stimulate interest that might, in some cases, lead to more intensive study.

Such a course should bring considerable prestige and favorable publicity, and would be a step toward fulfilling the admonition of the late Theodore Roosevelt, who once said: "I hold that every man owes something of his time and substance to the upbuilding of the profession or industry from which he gains his livelihood."

+ + +

95—"When the 'Better Light, Better Sight' program started to come into public prominence," writes a Canadian club executive, "we thought a meeting dedicated to this idea would take well. We talked it over with one of the largest manufacturers in the country. They willingly extended their co-operation by sending nearly $2,000 worth of equipment. A local power plant was contacted and happily installed two extra lines of power to handle the load. Another company, specializing in the formation of store windows, built a store window in the hotel ballroom. A large department store dressed the window. Local electrical shops put in displays, calling attention to this special meeting. So much could be seen that the papers took note and ran some interesting stories.

"Naturally, the meeting was an unusual success. So much so that next day three local merchants spent about $2,800 in improving their equipment!"

+ + +

96—Sponsoring civic movements of one sort or another is of course the natural province of the luncheon club. But why wait until some other organization has started something, and then "join in the chorus?" Look around, find some job that needs to be done, and make that your particular and exclusive responsibility. One club, for instance, has inaugurated an annual "Paint Up and Clean Up" week, in a middle western city. Much publicity has been given the project and the club has thus become definitely associated, in the public mind, with the whole "Paint Up and Clean Up" movement.

+ + +

97—"Never let a holiday pass without some sort of a celebration" is the policy of one live organization.

Usually, an element of humor is injected into these cele-
brations. On Valentine's Day, one member with some
"artistic" ability, collaborated with another, who did a
bit of scribbling. Together, they fixed up a set of comic
valentines, featuring club members. These were duly exhibited to the amusement of all—including the victims.

+ + +

98—Another example of a holiday celebration: One
club, last year, held an Armistice Day celebration. Members were asked to wear their army uniforms (if they
could possible get into them.) Responding to the usual
roll call, men who had seen service in the World War
gave the name of their company and division. Several
members recounted exciting or amusing war experiences.
A former army chaplain made an eloquent appeal for
peace and good-will among men. It was voted one of the
best meetings of the year.

+ + +

99—Probably you know, in a vague sort of way that
the Domestic Science departments of your high schools
train girls in the art of cooking. But you probably have
little conception of the thoroughness and excellence of
this training. Your local Board of Education would be
glad to co-operate in enlightening you, and the other
members of your organization. Why not arrange with

the Domestic Science Department of a high school to hold a meeting in the class-room, or to have a group of Domestic Science girls prepare and serve a meal in your club-room? They will be thrilled and delighted at the opportunity, and the experience should be mutually beneficial.

+ + +

100—One Canadian club held a very interesting session a few months ago. A special invitation was extended to all local ministers. The speaking period was divided into two parts, giving a Catholic priest twelve minutes and an Anglican Bishop an equal period of time. Entertainment was provided by musicians from the Salvation Army.

To enhance the church atmosphere eight boys were called upon to take up a collection. Each boy had a church plate in one hand, and wore a boxing glove on the other hand. They extracted $32.00 from the "congregation" in less than ten minutes. Then, the names of all ministers were put in a hat, one was drawn and that minister was given the entire proceeds to turn in at his church the following Sunday.

THE END

LaVergne, TN USA
17 November 2009
164444LV00009B/47/A